In Control

A Skill-Building Program for Teaching Young Adolescents to Manage Anger

WITHDRAWN

Millicent H. Kellner

Research Press
2612 North Mattis Avenue • Champaign, Illinois 61822
www.researchpress.com

Copies of this book may be ordered from Research Press at the address given on the title page.

Composition by Jeff Helgesen
Cover design by Linda Brown, Positive I.D. Graphic Design
Printed by Malloy Lithographing, Inc.

ISBN 0–87822–463–7

Library of Congress Catalog Number 00–109537

To the memory of my beloved parents, Samuel and Anne Kellner, who always extended a hand to be helpful to others

To Barbara Strickarz, whose steadfast vision, leadership, support, and concern for children made the development of this special program possible

Contents

Preface

It has been my pleasure to have served since 1986 as a school social worker at High Point Adolescent School in Morganville, New Jersey. A therapeutic day school set within an outpatient behavioral health care agency, High Point School includes an elementary school as well as an adolescent school, the latter serving youth aged 12 to 21 years with severe emotional, behavioral, and learning difficulties. These students have been classified as needing out-of-district special education by their local school districts and by New Jersey and federal law (i.e., IDEA 1990 and subsequent amendments).

In 1992, school staff at the High Point Adolescent School began to explore innovative, proactive methods to encourage prosocial skill development, especially approaches to anger control, in middle and high school aged students at the High Point Adolescent School. Initially, we focused on offering the anger management program in a small group format. We were encouraged by the results of the small group approach (Kellner & Tutin, 1995). Then we did a pilot study. Pretest and posttest assessment by teachers and parents on the conduct subscale of the Conners' Teacher and Parent Rating Scales (Conners, 1989) showed significant improvement, and a trend toward fewer incidents of physical aggression in school also emerged (Kellner & Bry, 1999).

We had encouraging results, but we still worried that, by definition, the small group approach might unfairly label some students as "troublemakers" while ignoring the needs of so many other students. Our answer to this dilemma was to move the anger management program into our classrooms. By teaching a whole class, we were able to destigmatize participation as well as reach more students. By focusing on students at a younger age (middle school rather than high school age), we hoped the program would be even more influential. Because we have such a strong clinical component in our adolescent school, the classroom program has been conducted by the school social worker, with the classroom teachers and teaching assistants as co-facilitators. When we compared a group of students who had "graduated" from the anger management program to a group who had been encouraged only to fill out anger logs but who had not participated in the program (Kellner, Colletti, & Bry, 1999), we found that anger management program participants had significantly fewer incidents of peer fighting and made significantly greater use of anger logs. We also found that program graduates more frequently initiated contact with the emergency clinician to talk about anger-related incidents.

After the program, 19 graduates received four monthly booster sessions. These participants continued to fill out significantly more anger logs during the 4-month follow-up period than did both graduates who did not receive the booster sessions and nonparticipants. Indeed, booster sessions clearly helped these participants maintain decreases in negative behavior and increases in prosocial coping. In short, whether they attended booster sessions or not, program graduates made consistent use of anger logs and strengthened the skills of self-awareness, self-evaluation, and planning ahead by writing about their angry responses.

In a further study (Kellner, Salvador, & Bry, 2001), we compared the observed classroom behavior of a group of participating students to a group of nonparticipants. In general, students who participated in the program were found to engage in more nonverbal and nonphysical positive/neutral behavior and, specifically, to engage in more positive/neutral behavior with their teachers. Most significantly, program participants exhibited a greater tendency to display the use of anger management skills (positive/neutral verbal and nonverbal behavior) in interactions with their teachers during structured classroom situations. Participants also showed less negative verbal and nonverbal behavior toward peers during unstructured classroom activity. This may indicate that, before generalizing the skills to other situations, they were best able to generate these new prosocial skills within the context of the structured situation in which the skills were taught. According to school incident reports, at the 3-month follow-up students in the program exhibited significantly fewer incidents involving aggression. Finally, along with our previous findings, the students who participated continued to make more significant use of their logs as a prosocial coping device for writing about their angry feelings than did students who did not participate.

Angry feelings are among the most difficult to control and channel appropriately; we can all benefit from developing and strengthening our anger management skills. As you probably know, students with severe emotional and behavioral challenges are more anger-prone—and more likely to tear up forms than to fill them out. Therefore, it is encouraging that such students can learn prosocial skills that may serve them well throughout their lives, given the opportunity in a structured, effective program that offers them the skills and incentives to cope appropriately and remain in control. Moreover, our results indicate that even students with less serious difficulties can benefit from the program. We wish you all the best in using these proven materials with all of your students.

Acknowledgments

This manual could not have been completed without the unwavering support and encouragement of many people: I am grateful to Juan Iglesias, Clinical Coordinator of High Point Schools, for giving me the opportunity to create this anger management program for children. My clinical colleagues at High Point School—Stephen Hecht, MSW, LCSW, and Alba Wagar, MSW, LCSW—provided exceptionally intelligent suggestions for developing this program. Thank you to the High Point Middle School teachers—Marilyn Eisenberg, Karen Muldoon, Loretta Nagy, Jacqueline Kelly, and Donna McDonald—who made ongoing suggestions that helped strengthen and improve the program. The secretarial and organizational assistance of Laura Siemientkowski and Cheryl Ernst has been priceless in bringing this work to completion. Laura Ann Coletti, once my doctoral student research assistant and now a school psychologist, provided invaluable help with the proofreading task.

Introduction

This program guide has been written with one purpose in mind: to help you teach young people effective anger management skills. Students with attention-deficit/hyperactivity disorder (AD/HD) and behavior disorders will benefit especially from the program, but the skills taught will be useful to everyone else in the school population as well. Geared toward adolescents of middle school age and intended primarily for in-class use, the sessions are readily adaptable for use in small group or individual contexts.

Research findings suggest that participation in the *In Control* anger management program can help students with emotional and behavioral difficulties reduce incidents of angry acting out and, through the use of cognitive-behavioral strategies, assist in the development of adaptive prosocial behavior. These results have been observed in both structured and unstructured settings, with teachers and peers, suggesting that the prosocial behavior learned in the program can generalize across situations.

In Control focuses on a child's relationship to his or her own feelings, and the program is geared toward helping children take an essential step in the development of interpersonal skills and relationships with others. As such, the program is not an intensive interpersonal skill development program, such as conflict resolution. Rather, it is a precursor to programs that emphasize the skills required to negotiate the needs of two different people in a relationship. Although the program makes extensive use of skill-building techniques that take place in an interpersonal context (e.g., role-play), the main goal is to help youngsters gain the awareness and skills to manage the unique, yet malleable, dimensions of their anger (physiology, thoughts, emotion, behavior) so they can achieve self-control and develop a repertoire of prosocial behaviors.

Flexibility is the key to conducting this program successfully. Although the material is divided into 10 sessions, to conduct over a period of 10 weeks, you can expand or modify the sessions to accommodate your schedule, unique classroom needs, or other factors. For example, in some schools, 45- to 60-minute sessions may be too long, given scheduling concerns and student attention spans. You can easily divide a session up. Or you might opt to spend more than 60 minutes on a session in response to high student enthusiasm and productivity. Use your professional judgment to make this program work for you and your students.

Ten Points in Anger Management

The *In Control* anger management program stresses the idea that problems arise not because people feel angry but because they choose inappropriate ways of responding to their anger. More specifically, the program works toward students' understanding of the following important points:

1. Anger is a normal and natural human feeling.

2. An anger *trigger* is a situation or event that sets us off.

3. An anger *setting* is a place where we tend to get angry.

4. An *anger log* helps us reflect on how we handled our anger this time and decide how we might handle it better next time.

5. Anger management helps us *recognize* our anger, *interrupt* ourselves before we act out our angry feelings, and then *substitute* an anger management tool.

6. Anger shows itself in our physiology (our bodies). Deep breathing, counting, and muscle relaxation are examples of *physiological tools* for anger management.

7. What we think to ourselves has an effect on how angry we get. Self-talk and self-statements are *thinking tools* for anger management.

8. What we choose to do can help us stay calm and in control. Walking away or talking things out with a friend are examples of *behavioral tools* for anger management.

9. When we manage anger well, we stay in control, respect people and property, and get positive results.

10. Anger management helps us make our anger work for us: We think ahead and make plans to stay calm and in control.

Appendix A1 lists these points in a reproducible form so you can provide students with individual copies. You might also want to make (or have students make) a poster for display during each session.

Session Format

Each of the 10 *In Control* anger management sessions includes the following components:

Goals statement: For leaders, specifies how the session will help students manage anger more effectively.

Objectives statement: For students, explains the specific purposes of the session.

Materials list: Lists the supplies and equipment you will need to run the session efficiently. For each session, you will need to have a way to display information in a whole-class format (e.g., overhead projector with blank transparencies, easel pad and markers).

Overview: Provides an introduction and background information to prepare you to teach more effectively.

Leader script: Recreates the content of the test-piloted sessions to guide your interactions with students. In this script, *leader dialogue* appears in plain type to indicate what you should say to students. (Feel free to put these ideas into your own words.) *Leader notes* appear in italics. These notes give you procedural instructions and additional information to keep students focused and the session running smoothly. *Key concepts* are interspersed throughout the leader script to help you stay focused on the session's main ideas.

Supplementary Materials

Connecting Activities

Connecting activities associated with the sessions establish a cross-curricular link between anger management and academic studies. These activities are optional but highly recommended. Why? Because they help reinforce and strengthen learning about anger management outside the sessions. They will help both you and your students integrate each session's anger management tips and information into an academic area. The range of activities will not only keep students interested but also speak to various learning styles. For example, a student who may find writing a paragraph difficult may get more out of drawing a picture or acting out a short drama. You can easily adapt these activities to your students' needs, abilities, and interests.

In addition, connecting activities provide opportunities to assess student understanding more authentically. For example, the essay written in the connecting activity for Session 9, "Things That Bug Me," will provide you with evidence of students' understanding of anger management skills as applied in their lives. Whenever writing is the form of expression called for, be sensitive to students who find writing difficult, whether for physical, emotional, or academic reasons. Consider accommodating these students' needs by offering alternative activities (e.g., art) or other communication methods (e.g., dictation). In all connecting activities, keep the focus on learning to manage anger better, rather than on academics.

Review Sheets

Each session (2 through 10, plus booster sessions) begins with your distributing and discussing a written review of events during the previous session. Reviewing the previous session creates a link between it and the present lesson and helps students consolidate the information they have learned.

In completing the review sheets, make every effort to preserve and describe the contributions made by *your* students—especially the lists your students generate (of anger triggers, anger management settings, and the like). For sessions involving role-playing, give credit to individual contributors and personalize the role-plays by including student names (first names or initials only if the sheets will be viewed by others and you are concerned about confidentiality). Personal recognition not only helps increase class participation but also supports student self-esteem.

Instructions for each session specify that you, as the teacher, are to prepare the review sheet for each session. However, you may also give students copies of the review sheet to fill out during the session, or ask them to complete the sheet as a homework assignment. Whenever possible, have another staff member observe the session and make notes as to what should appear on the session's review sheet. If a staff member is unavailable and it is appropriate for your class, you may consider rotating the "recording" role among the students.

Leader Checklists

A leader checklist at the end of each session gives you a way to monitor your performance and summarizes the anger management topics discussed. This summary will help you keep track of the specific topics you have been able to cover and those you may have omitted for a variety of reasons, including time pressures. As such, the checklist serves as a reminder to make up the omissions in subsequent sessions.

Student Anger Management Folders

Give each student a folder in which to keep review sheets, connecting activity work, anger logs, and other anger management materials. By the end of the program, each student will have a full summary of the anger management program to which he or she can refer. The materials will be personalized because they will reflect the unique contributions of this class and these students. You can also encourage students to personalize the outsides of their folders with artistic renderings of their names, anger management–related drawings, and the like. Finally, it is often helpful to use the folder contents to encourage students to take ownership of the program—for example, to praise them for the clear evidence of their hard work and knowledge.

The Anger Log: A Step-by-Step Approach

The anger log is an essential component of this anger management program. The log enables students to record a variety of aspects related to the incidents that have made them angry. Moreover, it promotes self-awareness and helps students learn to evaluate the degree to which they have successfully managed their anger. As students track incidents, they further practice successful anger management.

Ideally, students will ultimately use the log in a preventive fashion, filling it out before they have behaved aggressively. However, it is also very helpful for students to complete a log after they have behaved inappropriately because this provides an invaluable opportunity for them to practice the skills of self-awareness, self-evaluation, and planning ahead to bring about improved behavior in the future.

As is the case for many other anger management programs, the anger log is based on the "Hassle Log" originally developed by Feindler and Ecton (1986). The *In Control* log is unique, however, because it applies specifically to school settings and because the content evolves in increments, session by session. That is, as a new concept is introduced and students master it, it is added to the log. In addition, the log includes a section to help students decide whether or not they made their anger work for them and another to encourage them to plan ahead by considering how they might handle the same situation the next time it occurs. A sample copy of the log, as it appears when complete, is shown on the next page.

These modifications grew out of the desire to reinforce learning by giving students ample opportunity to think about, practice, and integrate each anger management concept and skill before moving on to the next one. Session 7 offers the complete anger log, reflecting all the basic anger management concepts and techniques. In Sessions 8, 9, and 10, students focus on practicing and internalizing their learning.

The Anger Log and Authentic Assessment

The anger log is useful for "authentic" assessment because it allows you and the student to observe whether he or she is applying anger management learning in a real-world context. By comparing early entries to later entries, you can also monitor student improvements in managing anger.

In the beginning, the students may tend to use the log *after* they have mismanaged anger. Over time, students may use the log as a coping behavior *before* they behave inappropriately. Considering this issue may also be worthwhile in authentic assessment.

Encouraging Anger Log Use

Encourage your students to use an anger log whenever they are angry. Make them readily available at a predetermined location in the classroom, perhaps a special place on your desk. Some teachers have increased students' cooperation in using and completing anger logs by offering a reward consistent with the classroom's rules of operation. For example, in classrooms using point systems, a student may earn a point for each log completed. Ten points might earn candy for the student, while 30 points might earn a gift certificate for

Sample Final Anger Log

Name _____Maurice R._____ Date ____April 10_____

What was your trigger?

- ❑ Somebody started fighting with me.
- ☑ Somebody teased me.
- ❑ Somebody insisted I do something.
- ❑ Somebody took something of mine.
- ❑ Somebody did something I didn't like.
- ❑ Other _____

Where were you when you got angry?

☑ School ❑ Neighborhood ❑ Home ❑ Other _____

How angry were you?

1	2	3	4	5
not angry	mildly angry	moderately angry	(4) really angry	burning mad

		How did you handle your anger?	How will you handle your anger next time?
Inappropriate responses	Yelling	❑	❑
	Throwing something	❑	❑
	Cursing	☑	❑
	Threatening someone	❑	❑
	Breaking something	❑	❑
	Hitting someone	❑	❑
	Other _____	❑	❑
Appropriate responses			
Physiological tools	Counting to 10, 20, 30	❑	☑
	Taking deep breaths	❑	❑
	Relaxing my muscles	❑	❑
	Other _____	❑	❑
Thinking tools	Using self-talk/self-statement	❑	❑

Write down what you thought or said to yourself.

Just because he's teasing me doesn't mean I have to lose it.

Stay calm.

Behavioral tools	Talking it out	❑	❑
	Ignoring it	❑	❑
	Going for a run	❑	❑
	Walking away	❑	❑
	Other _____	❑	❑

Did you make your anger work for you?

- ❑ Yes   I stayed in control, respected people and property, and had positive results.
- ☑ No   I lost control, hurt people or property, and/or had negative results.

How did you handle the situation?

1	2	3	4	5
poorly	(2) not so well	OK	well	great

lunch at the student's favorite fast-food restaurant. In short, staff should treat the logs and other class work associated with the anger management program in the same manner they would treat other class assignments.

Anger Log Management

Each classroom should develop its own system for working with and storing completed logs so students can compare their logs (and evaluate their behavior) over time. Many teachers have had students store their logs in their anger management folders. However, you may elect to hold on to the completed logs, especially if you use the improved behavior reflected in the log over time to reinforce students' application of anger management skills. For example, you could encourage Tomas to avoid being too self-critical about his recent incident of inappropriate cursing behavior because his logs show that, just 6 weeks ago, Tomas was hitting people when he was angry. In addition, it is helpful to examine each completed log to make sure students understand the principles of anger management and how to use the log. If you do decide to review and/or keep the logs, you should always fully respect the feelings of students who do not wish to share their logs with you. However, if students in a particular class are being rewarded for filling out logs, students who choose not to share logs should still be rewarded for filling them out.

Preparing for and Leading Sessions

To prepare for each session, read the goals and objectives statements, gather the materials listed, and study the overview. Duplicate the review sheet you will complete for your group, handouts (for the connecting activity and other purposes), and the leader checklist. Plan to write down significant concepts and record student responses in whatever whole-class format you have chosen. Writing and displaying this information reinforces learning and documents the information you will need to personalize the review sheet for each session. Plan to spend 45 to 60 minutes running each session, or adjust the time according to your own situation.

Anger Triggers and Settings

As you will see in the leader scripts, the program requires a high degree of facilitator-student interaction. Beginning with Session 1 and continuing through Session 10, students create and build upon a list of anger triggers and anger settings. In general, students cooperate with making lists of anger triggers, anger settings, and so forth. The interaction that takes place between you and the class in creating these lists gives you a wonderful opportunity to reinforce students' participation and contributions. In short, you support student self-esteem through such interaction.

Appendix A2 provides a list of common triggers and settings, handy if you want to suggest triggers and settings when your class appears to be running short of ideas. As sessions proceed, fewer new anger triggers and settings will emerge. However, you should always be prepared to add new contributions to the class list. Make a poster of anger triggers and settings to display during each session. You can transfer new items to the poster after each session, or you can ask a student volunteer to do so.

Leading Meaningful Discussions

To lead discussions in which each student feels comfortable contributing, follow these general guidelines:

▷ Accept all responses and keep judgmental comments to a minimum, at least initially. Instead, wait patiently for the student to come up with his or her own positive contributions, even if only loosely related. Record ideas in the whole-class format.

▷ Strongly reinforce students for participating. Make frequent encouraging comments, such as "Thank you" and "That's an interesting one."

▷ Say *results* or *outcomes* rather than *consequences* when discussing reasons for managing anger appropriately. Many students have come to associate the latter term with punishment.

▷ Carefully avoid criticizing students who mismanage anger. Rather, explain that learning any new skill takes practice. When anger is mismanaged, students simply need more practice. Focus on what a student might do *next* time if confronted with the same situation.

▷ As you go, encourage students to anticipate the triggers and settings that upset them. Help them understand that the goal of the *In Control* program is to give them the anger management tools that will work for *them* as individuals. In short, we want to put them in control of themselves.

A word of caution: Be prepared for students who maintain that physical violence is the only alternative. Always gently but firmly challenge such thinking by asking for a positive alternative. If the student cannot respond or be redirected, go on to another student. Most likely you will also encounter students who believe it is simply not possible to control their actions when they are angry. Respectfully question their thinking and try to redirect them. Avoid getting into power struggles, however. If a student is "stuck," move on to another student or other material.

Role-Playing

Role-playing is at the heart of the *In Control* program. As a device to simulate potential or actual anger-provoking events, role-playing helps people experience and examine their internal and external reactions to such events. Students, therefore, are provided with the opportunity to learn to identify and evaluate—in the safe setting of the classroom—their own unique physiological, cognitive, and behavioral responses when angry. Moreover, and perhaps most important, they can rehearse new and appropriate internal and external responses.

Hypothetical situations as well as reenactments of real-life situations can be the focus of role-plays. Indeed, initially, until students achieve a certain level of comfort with the program, you may need to use the sample role-plays included in the sessions. However, reenactments of actual student anger-related events provide the best learning opportunities. Students generally begin to volunteer such situations shortly after the program begins. Real events tend to involve students more fully; they also tend to ensure that the student's true reactions emerge during the role-play.

If in a given role-play a student has used good anger management skills, you have an excellent opportunity to praise the student. If the student shows an example of anger mismanagement, he or she has the chance to practice appropriate anger management, then apply the new strategy in real life. It is important to encourage all students to bring the anger management skills rehearsed in role-plays into everyday life outside the sessions. Praise students for the appropriate behavior you notice outside the session.

Step-by-step procedures for role-playing are given as Appendix A3. Because these procedures apply to role-plays across all sessions, you may want to copy this list for easy reference while you conduct the sessions.

A Word about Privacy

A question often arises about how to handle the personal and private nature of the situations students may choose to bring into the anger management sessions. Role-playing, general discussion, and other activities can expose students' personal business. While conducting a session, stay focused on teaching content within a psychoeducational framework. In other words, do not permit students to reveal material that is inappropriately intimate for the public setting of the classroom. Protect students from exposing too much of their private lives by stopping them if they begin to disclose potentially embarrassing content. Attend to the skill-building aspect and not to the details of the situation, then deal with personal concerns on an individual basis, referring students to other professionals for help if necessary.

Implementation Issues

By using this program, you can help your school create an environment in which everyone is familiar with the principles and language of anger management. Together, staff can give students the support they need to develop and maintain these skills. Certainly, the success of a school-based anger management program depends on providing students with ongoing opportunities to practice positive anger management skills throughout the school day. Therefore, use this book to train and familiarize *all* school staff with the anger management program so they will be able to support student skill development throughout the school: in the cafeteria, the gym, the playground, the hallways, and so forth.

Small Group and Individual Applications

Although this program is intended to be conducted by teachers, some school systems or individual schools might want their school psychologists and school social workers to be involved in running it. If this is the case, it nonetheless remains important for the classroom teacher to be present to help facilitate each session. One of the major benefits of the *In Control* program is that it takes place in the setting in which students regularly behave and react—the classroom. The classroom teacher is in the best position to witness anger-related incidents, reinforce the principles of anger management, and work toward shaping prosocial student behavior. Indeed, if the adult who spends the most time with the students in this setting conducts the program, students will benefit most.

As noted in the preface, another major benefit of conducting this program in the classroom is that children with behavioral difficulties are not pulled out of class to receive help and are therefore not stigmatized as "troublemakers" or "outsiders," an isolating situation that could harm their self-esteem. Furthermore, in a classroom program such children may have an enhanced opportunity for skill acquisition from positive peer role models.

Clearly, it may not always be possible to run classroom-based programs. Fortunately, it is easy to adapt and use the program for small groups and for individual counseling sessions held both inside and outside school settings. A group of six to eight students is optimal. To reduce the possibility of stigmatizing the group and to increase positive peer influences, ensure that participants exhibit a range of difficulty in managing anger, from mild to severe.

In individual sessions, the anger log may take on a more dominant role because more one-on-one time is available for discussing and analyzing relevant entries. Role-playing should still have a major place in the program, and individual counselors can join in role-playing with their young clients to support and model skill development.

Because skill development is the goal of the program, it is important that the significant others (e.g., teachers and parents) of the youth become familiar with the program's basic principles and vocabulary so they can help encourage, facilitate, and otherwise support skill acquisition. Whether you are providing small group or individual counseling, it is wise to hold an orientation session for all directly concerned with the youth's welfare, with the youth as a participant.

Booster Sessions

Booster sessions help support further skill development and promote maintenance of acquired skills after the program's 10 sessions are over. Specifically, booster sessions will help you do as follows:

▷ Monitor log use.

▷ Review, usually through role-playing, prosocial anger management strategies and techniques used since the last booster session.

▷ Reinforce prosocial behavior through the praise and encouragement of both staff and classmates.

▷ Identify additional anger-related issues for individual students or the class as a whole.

▷ Help students formulate, usually through role-playing, further anger management strategies and techniques.

Ideally, after a 2-week hiatus, offer booster sessions every other week for the rest of the school year. Minimally, hold booster sessions once a month. The two sample booster sessions offered in Appendix B will help you get started. After these first two sessions, you can create your own.

Evaluation

The *In Control* Anger Management Pretest/Posttest (in Appendix C) is helpful in evaluating how much students have learned from the program. If you administer the pretest before Session 1, you will obtain a baseline of student knowledge about the basic terms and concepts prior to instruction. You can also give this test after students have completed Sessions 1 through 10 of the program. You will then be able to compare and evaluate the degree to which students have learned the basic tenets of anger management.

Broadening the Program's Reach

Good anger management is something that should extend beyond students in classrooms. Involving all school staff in the *In Control* anger management program can help create the climate in which these skills may be learned more quickly and, of course, generalized. With all staff working together, students can be supported and encouraged as they practice new prosocial behaviors outside the session. Appendix D, "Organizing a Schoolwide Nonviolence Week," offers a number of ideas for undertaking this challenge.

A Final Word

We hope your students will find this learning process as interesting, challenging, and fun as ours have. Best wishes, then, for a successful anger management program—and improved student behavior based on putting students in control of themselves.

Anger Is a Normal Human Feeling

Goals

▷ To promote students' understanding that it is important to develop skills to get along with people from diverse backgrounds and cultures

▷ To help students learn that anger is a normal and powerful human emotion that can work for them if they manage it appropriately

Objectives

▷ Learning that no two people are alike and that differences can either be enjoyed or cause disagreements

▷ Appreciating that anger is a powerful but normal human emotion

▷ Considering the fact that positive ways of dealing with anger usually are better than negative ones and that positive responses make for good relationships and good feelings

▷ Recognizing that, through good anger management, it is possible to make anger work for you instead of against you

Materials

▷ Easel pad (or another whole-class format)

▷ Student anger management folders (one per student)

▷ Connecting activity: Handout (one per student)

▷ *In Control:* Ten Points in Anger Management (Appendix A1; one per student)

Overview

Engaging students in the program begins in the first session. Students are usually surprised to hear that anger is a normal feeling that can work for them instead of against them. Indeed, some students have been disciplined so often, due to the inappropriate intensity of their anger and the behavior accompanying their anger, that they have concluded that anger itself is "bad." This session helps such students understand that problems come from *mismanaged* anger, not from anger itself. Normalizing anger is, therefore, a basic foundation of this program.

When you help normalize anger, you can more effectively encourage students to acknowledge, rather than deny, this emotion. Moreover, you will validate their angry feelings. Both steps are necessary to help youth begin to identify and deal with their anger and anger arousal levels.

Leader Script

Greet students, introducing yourself and asking their names, if necessary.

Session Content

The *In Control* program is designed to help you learn how to manage your anger. In this first session, we'll talk about why it's important to develop skills to get along with all kinds of different people. We'll talk about how having angry feelings is normal. It's important to admit these strong feelings so you can begin to handle them in more appropriate and helpful ways.

Give each student a copy of the In Control: *Ten Points in Anger Management handout (Appendix A1). Explain that during the course of the program, these important points will be covered. If you wish, prepare (or ask a student to prepare) a poster listing these points. Display the poster at every session; refer to it as appropriate.*

No two people are alike.

No two people are alike—not in the way they look on the outside and not in the way they look at things from the inside. How might people be different?

Pause for responses, recording them as students speak; sample answers include how people look and talk, what ideas they have, what religion they practice.

These differences make each of us unique. They also make life interesting. What a dull world it would be if all of us were exactly the same! So as we go through life, we can count on meeting people who are as different from us as winter is from summer.

Often the differences between people lead to many positive things: variety, alternatives, choices, and options. Can you think of any more positive examples?

Pause for responses, recording them as students speak.

From our differences come teams of specialists who work together to solve problems. For example, a basketball team has two forwards, two guards, and one center. Each position has a specific job to do so that together the team can score points. Differences can make us stronger when we work together.

Differences can also enrich our lives. Because our country has opened its doors to people from all over the world, we are exposed to many different and interesting cultures that remind us how diverse humankind is. But how might these differences between people lead to disagreements and misunderstandings?

Pause for responses, recording them as students speak; sample answers include not understanding a person's reasons for doing or not doing something, assuming other people think the same way you do, misunderstanding someone's intentions.

As you grow up and become adults, it becomes more and more important to learn to handle these disagreements and misunderstandings in a nonviolent, effective manner. To do this, each person needs to be able to *manage* his or her own angry feelings.

Anger is a normal human feeling.

How many of you have been angry? If so, raise your hand.

Raise your hand, too. If anyone indicates he or she has never been angry, pause briefly. Smile at the person or persons and continue.

We've all been angry at one time or another. Sometimes, though, young people have the idea that teachers, parents, and other adults disapprove of their angry feelings. Other young people have learned to expect to have to push their anger back down inside them. Still others may believe no one takes their angry feelings seriously.

A major goal of the *In Control* anger management program is to help you understand that anger is a normal human feeling that, like your other feelings, you need to manage in a socially appropriate manner. More often than not, it is the way a person handles his or her anger—not being angry itself—that leads to negative outcomes.

When you understand and accept that anger is a normal human feeling, you will have taken the important first step toward becoming comfortable admitting to yourself that you are angry. You will be able to do this without denying your angry feelings or expressing them in a negative way, such as fighting with someone.

What might you say to someone when your anger is out of control?

Pause for responses, recording them as students speak; sample answers include "I'll do whatever I want!" and "I hate you!" If students offer a curse as an example, you may just record the response as "curse" without writing down the inappropriate word or words.

How might you feel?

Record students' responses; sample answers: You feel like a volcano about to explode. You feel "pumped up." You feel sick to your stomach.

Being out of control might feel good to some kids, especially being "pumped up" and getting vengeance. In this program, however, you will practice staying in control and speaking calmly to adults or other students when you are angry. What could you say to express your anger in a way that showed you were in control?

Pause for and record responses; sample answers: "Yes, I'm angry about this and would like to talk through this disagreement" or, simply, "Let's talk this out."

What do you think you might do to control the way your body feels?

Pause for responses; sample answers: take deep breaths, count to 10. If students cannot answer, give them an example and tell them you will have more to say on the subject later.

Anger is a powerful feeling.

Anger is a powerful feeling. Because we feel anger so strongly, there is always the danger that our anger will control us instead of that we will control our anger. Skillful anger management will help you keep your body and mind calm when you feel very, very angry. In turn, this will help you think more clearly and behave more responsibly.

It is best to manage your anger in a positive way.

Why is it better to manage your angry feelings? What can happen if you don't manage your anger appropriately?

Guide the discussion to include the following points.

When anger is not managed well, or *mismanaged*, the result can be as mild as unnecessary misunderstandings between people or as severe as harm coming to a person or property. Often an angry person who is out of control winds up with some type of a negative result, such as losing a privilege or a friendship, suffering some other punishment, or simply losing self-respect and feeling embarrassed for not being in control.

Let's discuss some of the problems with mismanaged anger. Why do you think we use terms such as "losing it" to describe mismanaged anger?

Pause for responses; sample answer: You "lose" your self-control.

Yet growing up has to do with assuming more responsibility for our lives and being in control of ourselves, our thoughts, our feelings, and our behavior. Other people are more likely to respond positively to our concerns when we manage our anger in socially appropriate ways. Good anger management leads to good interpersonal relationships. This means that learning to manage anger helps us get along better with other people.

You can use your anger to work for you, not against you.

Like all human feelings, anger gives us important information about our own experiences. In this sense, our feelings—including our angry feelings—are signals that guide our actions and reactions to people and situations in the world around us. Many times, anger appears because someone has hurt us or been disrespectful to us. That is why people sometimes cry when they are angry. Crying becomes a way to express anger as well as hurt.

What do you do now to stay in control and handle your anger in a socially appropriate way?

> *Pause for responses, recording them as students speak. Sample answers: count to 10, breathe deeply, listen to music, walk away, talk things out with a friend. (If necessary, remind students that you are asking for appropriate ways only.)*

As you learn to manage your anger, you will develop more nonviolent strategies for appropriately expressing and coping with your angry feelings. This means you will learn to make your anger work *for* you, not *against* you. Believe it or not, your anger will become an ally, or friend, to help you reach a specific goal in a constructive way. If you think managing your anger in a positive way is difficult, you are not alone. It is. Just because you don't know something now doesn't mean you can't learn it. That's what this program is all about.

Closing

> *Distribute the student anger management folders, then explain the following.*

We are going to have nine more meetings to discuss anger management. Each of you will have your own folder in which to save materials from these sessions. In addition, we will begin each new meeting with a review of our previous session by reading a review sheet. The review sheet will be a record of the main anger management principles we learned and discussed in the meeting before. It will also be a record of your own thoughts and responses.

By the end of the program, we will learn a lot about how the people in this particular class handle anger now and how they learn to handle it, over time, as we meet. We'll make special lists of this class's reactions, thoughts, and ideas. And as we meet, we will keep adding to our lists.

Please keep all of the review sheets and other materials in your folder as a running account of the hard and thoughtful work you are doing in this class. At the next session, we will start talking about some good techniques to help you manage what's going on in your bodies when you feel angry.

> *Praise students for their participation, then let them know the date and time for the next session.*

Connecting Activity

Language Arts

Give each student a connecting activity handout. Review the instructions as a group. Answer any questions students may have. Process this activity a few days later during language arts time. You could also share one or two essays during review time at the beginning of Session 2 or treat the activity like homework: Read the essays and write supportive comments to help establish a positive one-on-one relationship with individual students. For students who find writing difficult, offer the option of dictation.

Connecting Activity

Name _____ Date _____

Write a paragraph describing how you manage your anger right now. Decide whether you think you need to make changes in your present style of managing your anger. Explain why you think you should or should not change your present style.

_____

_____

_____

_____

_____

_____

_____

_____

_____

_____

_____

_____

_____

_____

_____

_____

_____

_____

_____

_____

_____

_____

_____

Review

Name _____ Date _____

1. **No two people are alike.**

   This is positive because individual differences are interesting, and we wouldn't want everyone to be the same. Differences can be a problem, however, when they cause disagreements and fights.

2. **Anger is a *normal* human feeling.**

   Everyone gets angry.

   What matters is *how* you manage your anger.

   You don't need to feel bad if you don't already know how to manage your anger. You can learn.

3. **Anger is a *powerful* feeling.** Anger is powerful, but you can stay in control. When a person gets out of control, here are some things we said he or she might say or do.

   _____

   _____

   _____

   _____

   _____

4. **Staying calm and in control.** In this program, we want to help you make your anger work *for* you, not against you. What do the members of our class do to stay in control and handle anger in a positive and socially appropriate way?

   _____

   _____

   _____

5. **Program organization.** Week by week, you'll learn about the many anger management tools in this program. We'll have a review sheet for each session. If you keep all these sheets in your anger management folder, at our last session you'll have a very useful summary of the whole program.

   _____

   _____

   _____

6. **Other comments**

   _____

   _____

   _____

Please save this review sheet in your anger management folder.

ANGER IS A NORMAL HUMAN FEELING

Leader Checklist

Leader name _____   Date of session _____

I covered the following topics today *(check all that apply)*.

1. We all get angry.

   ❏ Told students that no two people are alike.

   ❏ Described anger as a normal human feeling.

   ❏ Described anger as a powerful feeling.

2. Anger can work for or against you.

   ❏ Discussed with students that mismanaged anger can lead to many problems and listed some of these.

   ❏ Told students that they can learn to use their anger to work *for* them.

   ❏ Discussed and listed methods students use now for staying in control and handling anger in a socially appropriate manner.

3. Classroom management issues:

   ❏ Explained that there will be nine more meetings (ten total).

   ❏ Distributed a student anger management folder to each member of the class and discussed how it will be used.

   ❏ Explained the role of the review sheet.

4. I also covered the following area(s).

   _____

   _____

   _____

Anger Log/Physiology of Anger

Goals

▷ To help students learn about the physiology of anger

▷ To encourage awareness of the benefits of the anger log, a tool for evaluating anger and planning for change

Objectives

▷ Recognizing how awareness of the physiology of anger (bodily responses to angry feelings) can help one stay calm and in control

▷ Learning three anger management techniques to control physiological responses to anger: counting, deep breathing, and muscle relaxation

▷ Understanding that the anger log is a handy tool for seeing, evaluating, and planning how to handle one's anger

▷ Identifying the steps in good anger management: recognizing anger, interrupting anger before acting out inappropriately, and substituting an appropriate anger management tool

Materials

▷ Easel pad (or another whole-class format)

▷ Student anger management folders

▷ Session 1 review sheet (one per student)

▷ Anger Log 1 (one per student)

▷ Optional

Audiotape or CD player

Recording of soothing music or other relaxing sounds

▷ Connecting activity (Part 1)

Poster of the cardiorespiratory system

Drawing paper

Markers or colored pencils

▷ Connecting activity (Part 2)

If you choose to do Part 2 of the connecting activity with the class, arrange ahead of time to have the school nurse visit the class with a blood pressure cuff. If the school nurse is unavailable, perhaps a parent who is a nurse will volunteer.

Overview

As you review Session 1, you have another opportunity to normalize anger. You may find that some students are now interested in discussing this concept further, giving you another opportunity to differentiate the characteristics of mismanaged anger from those of well-managed anger. Most important, however, you can show students you will support their efforts to identify and acknowledge their angry feelings.

This session introduces the anger log, an anger management tool that students can use to gain a deeper understanding of the factors involved in an angry incident and to evaluate the success of their anger management strategies. When students can evaluate their responses in one situation, they can make plans to improve the next time. Anger logs also link the sessions and situations in everyday life more closely. If you and/or the students keep the completed logs, they can show the development of anger management skills over time.

When introducing the anger log, explain that it will develop in increments that reflect the skills students are learning and that after Session 7 the log will be complete. Let students know where they may pick up copies of the log. You or an administrator at your school may want to send a letter to parents telling them that students may bring the logs home if they wish to do so.

Emphasize that, along with other anger management techniques, the anger log is an important tool to add to students' anger management "toolbox." Encourage students to use the log daily to record their successes as well as their struggles in anger management. This means that they may, especially in the beginning, fill out logs after they have mismanaged an angry event. Ultimately, you will guide them to fill out logs as a way of coping before they behave aggressively.

Do not criticize students who mismanage their anger. Rather, stress the importance of practicing new skills in order to master them. Therefore, encourage students to use the log to record how they handled their anger "this time" as well as how they intend to handle it "next time." If they handled themselves well, this will be reinforcing. If they mismanaged their anger, this will help them conceptualize and visualize effective anger management steps to apply in the future. Be prepared for the student who insists that physical violence is the only alternative. Ask for a positive alternative. If the student is "stuck," move on to another student or other material.

In general, students are skilled at identifying the physiological signs of anger. How much they enjoy the relaxation exercise in this session, though, depends on the class culture. Some classes truly like the experience, whereas others resist and complain. Nonetheless, it is important that students understand and, whenever possible, experience the difference between the tense and the relaxed body.

Leader Script

Review

Greet students warmly and give each a completed Session 1 review sheet, prepared in advance.

In the first meeting we explained that anger is a normal human feeling. But it's still important to learn how to manage anger effectively. The *In Control* program is designed to help you learn about handling your angry feelings in a positive way that puts you in control of yourself. Good anger management can improve communication between people and can help us avoid negative results, such as violence and punishment.

Let's take turns reading the Session 1 review sheet aloud to help you remember the main points from the last session.

Ask for volunteers. Be sensitive to those who may be embarrassed about reading aloud. For example, you could ask a reluctant student to share one thing he or she found interesting or helpful in the last session. Remind students to keep their review sheets in their anger management folders.

Session Content

Anger creates physiological responses.

As you learn the skills of anger management, you will also learn special concepts (ideas) and a special vocabulary. Anger has its own physiology. *Anger physiology* refers to the many ways in which anger shows itself in our bodies.

Being aware of anger physiology helps you remain in control in many important ways. First, you can better recognize and acknowledge your anger. Second, you can better recognize the signs of anger in other people. Most important, you can use your knowledge of your own anger physiology to keep yourself calm and in control when you feel angry. You can't make good decisions unless you're calm and in control of yourself.

Let's make a list of some of the signs you feel in your body when you are angry.

Pause for and record responses; sample answers: shallow breathing, tight muscles, rapid heartbeat, "pounding" head, churning stomach.

Everyone has these kinds of reactions when angry, even though one person may get a headache and another's heart may beat rapidly. If you feel these reactions, it's completely normal.

Physiological tools help you manage your body's responses to anger.

It helps to learn about and practice certain physiological techniques to manage your body's responses to anger and keep yourself calm and in control. We call these *physiological tools*. Practicing these techniques will prepare you to manage your responses when you are actually angry. The first physiological tool is counting. Let's try it.

Counting

Let's count slowly to 10 together. First, count forward: 1, 2, 3. . . . Next, count backward: 10, 9, 8. . . . What physiological responses did you observe in your own body? Let's list these.

Pause for responses, recording them as students speak; sample answers: more relaxed, breathing slowed, thinking became clearer.

Deep breathing

Now let's try another approach, deep breathing: All together, let's take three very deep breaths.

You should participate fully in this exercise. Take three deep breaths along with students.

What physiological responses did you observe in your own body? Let's list these, too.

Pause for responses; sample answers similar to those for counting.

Muscle relaxation

A third technique is muscle relaxation. Now I am going to lead what we call a relaxation exercise. I understand that some of you may feel a little uncomfortable about doing this kind of thing, but let's take this seriously because it really can help you feel better.

If desired, put on a CD or audiotape of relaxing sounds or soothing music. Dim the lights. As you give directions, participate as fully as you can in this exercise, too.

Now, sitting in your seats and keeping your eyes closed, stretch out your arms and extend your hands. Beginning with your fingers, hands, wrists, forearms, and biceps, all the way up to your shoulders, tense your muscles as tightly as you can. Feel the tension from your fingertips all the way to your shoulders. Hold it. Hold it. Make your arms as tense as you can. Hold on to the tension for 5 seconds: 1 . . . 2 . . . 3 . . . 4 . . . 5.

Now, let's relax those muscles, one muscle group at a time. Beginning with your fingers and working up to your shoulders, feel the relaxation after you "untense" each muscle group. Hold on to that relaxed feeling. Think about how good it feels.

Next, focus on your legs, remembering to keep your eyes closed. Beginning with your toes, create tension all the way up to your thighs. Hold on to the tension for 5 seconds: 1 . . . 2 . . . 3 . . . 4 . . . 5. Now relax your legs. Hold on to the relaxed feeling. Think about how good it feels.

You may need to remind students to keep their eyes closed.

Now relax your legs. How does that feel?

Finally, let's repeat the tension-relaxation procedure with the muscles in your face. Begin at your chin and work up to your forehead. Feel the tension. Hold on to the tension for 5 seconds: 1 . . . 2 . . . 3 . . . 4 . . . 5. Now relax your face. Think about how good it feels.

Now take three more deep breaths and slowly open your eyes.

Give the students a few moments to reorient themselves, then ask the following questions.

Who can describe the feeling of tensing your muscles? *(tightness, soreness, pressure on the chest, difficulty breathing)*

How did it feel to relax your muscles? *(loose, easier to breathe, restful)*

Who has any further observations to share or comments to make about the contrast they felt between tension and relaxation?

Encourage students to describe their own personal responses to these two states.

It is very helpful to practice counting, deep breathing, and muscle relaxation. When you feel angry, you can *interrupt* your angry response before you act out inappropriately and *substitute* the anger management techniques of counting, deep breathing, and/or muscle relaxation. The more you practice using these physiological tools, the more you will find you automatically use them when you feel bodily tension, including the tension that goes with your anger. The three methods we practiced today are handy tools you can carry with you at all times. They are ready substitutes to help you manage your anger better and remain in control.

An anger log helps you see, evaluate, and plan how you handle your anger.

Give a blank copy of Anger Log 1 to each student.

An *anger log* is a tool to help you see, evaluate (judge), and plan the way you handle your anger. Each week I will give you a new version of the anger log to keep in your anger management folders. We will keep extra anger logs *(name a central location)*. You may use an anger log whenever you are angry: to help you handle anger well or when you need more practice managing your anger.

Instead of specifying a central location, you may distribute more blank logs during the session. Students may keep their completed anger logs, or you may identify a central drop-off location for these, too. If you choose this last option, bear in mind privacy issues.

Plus, you will see that the log grows every week as we discuss new concepts and learn new skills. At each session, the new approaches you've learned will be added to the log. This time, the log focuses on the three techniques you learned today. When you fill out the log, you have the opportunity to discover which technique works best for *you*.

Like all new learning experiences, anger management will take practice. Remember, everyone makes mistakes while learning. Do you see the examples of anger mismanagement on the log's list of possible behaviors?

Ask for volunteers to take turns reading these examples.

This list will help if you honestly examine *all* your behavior—both appropriate and inappropriate. Now find and circle the three physiological tools on the log I gave you.

Check to ensure each student sees where and how to record techniques used. It may be helpful to fill out a sample log as a group, using a volunteer's memory of an incident or a hypothetical situation.

Good anger management involves recognizing, interrupting, and substituting.

Let's put it all together now: For good anger management, you (a) *recognize* your anger, (b) *interrupt* yourself before you behave inappropriately, then (c) *substitute* an appropriate anger management tool to calm yourself and stay in control. That is, you substitute bodily relaxation, calming thoughts, and calm behavior for angry behavior.

You can do it! It may take some practice—all the skills you learn take practice. If you practice the anger management skills we learn here outside the sessions, you will automatically be able to stay calm and in control, even when you are very mad.

Closing

In this session, we talked about some specific things you can do to control the physiological, or bodily, responses you have to anger. You also learned about the anger log, which we will be using from now on. Finally, we introduced the idea that the steps in managing anger are to recognize you're angry, interrupt your angry reaction, and substitute an appropriate anger management tool, in this case a physiological one.

For next time, fill out the anger log if you find yourself in a situation where you get angry. Try using one of the physiological tools to stay calm and in control. Filling out the anger log will give you the opportunity to find out exactly which physiological tools work best for you.

The next session will focus on anger triggers and settings that tend to provoke your anger.

Instruct students to put their review sheets and anger logs in their folders. Remind them of the central location to pick up more copies of the log.

Connecting Activity

Part 1: Art/Health

Display the poster of the cardiorespiratory system, and pass out drawing paper and art supplies. (If feasible, consider offering 3-D art materials, such as clay, as an alternative.) Instruct students as follows.

You have learned that anger has its own physiology. The physical changes that take place in your body involve the heart, lungs, and skin. Do you think your organs are working more or less hard when you are angry? Draw a picture of your heart, lungs, and skin undergoing the changes that come about when you are angry.

After students have had time to draw, give them an opportunity to share their drawings with the group.

Part 2: Health/Math and Science

Invite the school nurse to bring a blood pressure cuff to class and to explain what blood pressure readings mean.

Let's ask the nurse to measure our blood pressure when we are calm.

Have the nurse measure several students' blood pressure (all if possible). Record these numbers in a whole-class format.

Now, think of a time you were really, really angry, and have the nurse measure your blood pressure again.

Record these numbers in a whole-class format.

How does your blood pressure while you're in a calm state compare with your blood pressure while you're in an angry state?

Discuss the difference between blood pressure when calm and blood pressure when angry. If desired, you could repeat this exercise and have students keep a record of changes in their blood pressure over time. This would open up the possibility for charting, graphing, and the like.

Anger Log 1

Name _____ Date _____

		How did you handle your anger?	How will you handle your anger next time?
Inappropriate responses	Yelling	❏	❏
	Throwing something	❏	❏
	Cursing	❏	❏
	Threatening someone	❏	❏
	Breaking something	❏	❏
	Hitting someone	❏	❏
	Other _____	❏	❏
Appropriate responses			
Physiological tools	Counting to 10, 20, 30	❏	❏
	Taking deep breaths	❏	❏
	Relaxing my muscles	❏	❏
	Other _____	❏	❏

Review

Name _____ Date _____

1. **Physiology of anger.** The *physiology of anger* is the way anger shows itself in your body. Physical signs of anger are natural and universal (everyone experiences them). Our class said these physiological signs can tell a person he or she is angry.

   _____

   _____

   _____

2. **Physiological tools.** Controlling your physiological responses requires using physiological tools to help you calm down, relax, and remain in control. We discussed three: counting, deep breathing, and muscle relaxation.

   Counting and deep breathing can help you slow down so you have time to think. How did you feel after you practiced these techniques?

   _____

   _____

   _____

   Muscle relaxation means tensing and then relaxing your body, one set of muscles at a time. How does a tense body feel?

   _____

   _____

   _____

   How does a relaxed body feel?

   _____

   _____

   _____

3. **Good anger management.** In good anger management, you *recognize* your anger, *interrupt* your angry reaction before you act out inappropriately, then *substitute* an appropriate anger management tool to keep yourself calm and in control.

4. **Anger log.** The *anger log* is another anger management tool, designed to help you see, evaluate, and plan your anger management. The log will grow each week as you learn new skills and concepts. This session's anger log focused on inappropriate ways of reacting when you are angry and physiological tools you might use instead.

5. **Other comments**

   _____

   _____

   _____

Leader Checklist

Leader name _____ Date of session _____

I covered the following topics today *(check all that apply)*.

1. Review

    ❏ Reminded students that anger is a normal but powerful feeling.

    ❏ Restated the goals of the anger management program.

    ❏ Listed good reasons for managing anger appropriately.

2. Introduction to the physiology of anger

    ❏ Discussed anger physiology and listed physiological signs that indicate we are angry.

    ❏ Listed and discussed physiological tools that grow out of awareness of physiological signs of anger.

    ❏ Illustrated the use of physiological tools: counting, taking deep breaths, muscle relaxation.

    ❏ Conducted muscle relaxation exercise.

3. Introduction to the anger log

    ❏ Distributed the anger log and explained that it would develop incrementally by adding new ideas and skills each session.

    ❏ Explained that using the log is a way of seeing and evaluating how well we handle anger this time so we can plan a better way next time.

    ❏ Asked students to use the log to discover which physiological tools are most effective for them as individuals.

4. I also covered the following area(s).

    _____

    _____

Anger Triggers and Settings

Goals

▷ To encourage students to identify their own anger triggers and settings

▷ To help students learn how their anger triggers and settings relate to the frequency and intensity of their angry responses

Objectives

▷ Learning what one's individual anger triggers are and identifying settings in which controlling anger may be difficult

▷ Understanding that knowing one's own anger triggers and settings can be of help in managing anger appropriately

▷ Through role-playing, practicing the use of physiological anger management techniques

Materials

▷ Easel pad (or another whole-class format)

▷ Poster board and markers (for the triggers and settings poster)

▷ Student anger management folders

▷ Session 2 review sheet (one per student)

▷ Anger Log 2 (one per student)

▷ Connecting activity: Handout (one per student)

Overview

The focus of this session is anger triggers and settings: Students identify their own anger triggers and settings and have the opportunity to create a poster to which they will add as the sessions continue. Affirm each contribution! As students share ideas, ask for a show of hands regarding who else, staff included, could identify with each trigger. For your reference, a list of commonly mentioned triggers and settings appears as Appendix A2.

This session also introduces students to role-playing, a technique that will be used throughout the remainder of the program. Afraid your students won't buy into a role-play activity? Once one or two students agree to participate, other students will probably be eager to get involved. Before role-playing, be sure to review "Procedures for Role-Playing" (Appendix A3). These procedures apply to all sessions in which role-playing is a part. You will want to make a photocopy of this page for easy reference. Specific questions for the role-players appear in this and following sessions.

Because the *In Control* Program is intended primarily for classroom use, role-playing is structured to involve as many students as possible in the learning experience. The student who volunteers a situation to role-play becomes its "creator" (and, most commonly, director). This student provides a thumbnail sketch of the situation in which his or her anger was triggered. As other students role-play the event, they follow this general description but choose their own anger management tools and react and interact in their own ways. Follow-up questions after the role-play provide structure and involve students in an active discussion and dialogue.

Encourage the whole class to become involved in analyzing the anger management principles demonstrated in the role-playing situation. In this particular session, the focus is on the physiology of anger, the area of anger management covered in Session 2. Your goal is for the students to know how to use a physiological technique. If some students report that the technique did not work for them, that is fine. This presents a wonderful opportunity to remind students that every technique does not work for everyone and that anger management will introduce them to many tools. In the end, they must discover the tools that work best for them. Personalize the role-play on the session's review sheet by summarizing the situation and identifying the creator/director and actors by their names or initials.

Finally, this session's anger log adds a section to help students practice identifying anger triggers. Because it is often helpful to make students aware of the context (or setting) in which their anger is being aroused, the log includes the question "Where were you when you got angry?" Answering this question will help students assess whether there is a pattern to the settings in which they get "triggered." This, in turn, will help them recognize that they need a sound plan for dealing with situations in these anger-inducing settings. They may also learn that, because of previous negative experiences, they associate anger with certain places and therefore have a "shorter fuse" in these settings.

A note of caution: When you introduce the concept of an "anger trigger," at least one student will probably remark, evoking a violent theme, that firearms have triggers. This is an opportunity to help expand your students' general knowledge and vocabulary by pointing out that the word *trigger* has several meanings. One meaning refers to a device used to release or activate a mechanism, which applies to guns and many other objects, such as drills and circular saws. The word *trigger* in anger management means the situation that presses on us and leads us to release an angry reaction. In anger management, the *trigger* is the event that causes an angry reaction.

Leader Script

Review

Greet the students warmly. Distribute the Session 2 review sheet, prepared in advance. Have students take turns reading the parts of the review sheet aloud and discuss.

How many of you found using the anger logs helpful? Raise your hands.

Pause briefly, acknowledging the show of hands. Let one or two students explain how the log was helpful.

Who can tell me what the purpose of the anger log is?

Answer: a tool to help you see, evaluate, and plan your use of anger management skills so you can become aware of how you reacted this time and plan what to do next time.

Since the last session, has anyone had an opportunity to use a physiological tool to help you manage your anger? Which of the physiological tools were the most helpful to you?

Allow several students to share briefly.

Session Content

The focus of this session is anger triggers and settings. To help show you what I mean, let's consider the following situation:

At lunch time in the cafeteria, Steve teased Jonas about his height. Jonas was very angry, but he interrupted his angry reaction and substituted a physiological tool: He counted to 10 and took some deep breaths. He felt his muscles relax, and he began to walk away. Jonas stayed calm and in control. Steve saw that Jonas was leaving and said, "Hey, man, don't go. I was just kidding."

An anger trigger is a situation or event that provokes your anger.

Jonas managed to avoid getting into a fight by counting and taking some deep breaths before he replied. Later on, he was also able to identify what set him off. What do you think that was?

Answer: being teased about his height.

Today we are going to discuss anger triggers. An anger trigger is a situation or event that sets us off and provokes our anger. Jonas's anger trigger was being teased about his height. Who among us would have been angry like Jonas?

Pause for a show of hands: "Sure, none of us likes to be teased."

Can you name some other examples of anger triggers?

Allow a few students to share; acknowledge their ideas.

How do you feel about your triggers and being "triggered?"

Pause for responses, recording them as students speak. Sample answers: helpless, out of control, angry, upset, thinking no one else could possibly understand my triggers, feeling ashamed that I even have that trigger.

It is normal for us to feel these ways about triggers. However, when people get the opportunity to share their triggers with others, they usually learn that they have many triggers in common. This means that most people would get angry if faced with these triggers. Remember, being angry is not the problem. Anger is a normal human feeling. Instead, the problem is not handling the anger appropriately.

Let's make a list of triggers. As we do this, let's have a show of hands *(including staff)* for the triggers that apply to each of us. We'll add to this list every session, so we'll have a complete list of this group's triggers when we're done.

Record the settings students mentioned previously on the poster under the heading "Triggers," then ask for more, recording these as well.

Knowing your triggers will help you manage your anger better.

As of this session, the anger logs will include an "anger triggers" section.

Distribute copies of Anger Log 2; point out the triggers section.

The anger log now asks you to notice and record what triggers your anger as you continue to practice using physiological tools to keep yourself calm and in control. If you know the kinds of things that bother you, you won't be taken by surprise when an anger trigger happens.

Noticing settings that are challenging for you can help you stay calm and in control.

Now let's consider the places, or settings, in which you tend to become angry. After the incident in the cafeteria, Jonas realized that being in that particular place, the cafeteria, made him especially tense because it was so noisy and because he could encounter boys from other classes who did not know him well and might judge him solely by his height. He made an effort to stay calm and in control by making a conscious decision to keep his muscles relaxed before entering the cafeteria at lunch time.

Direct students to the question on the anger log about setting.

Also in this session, the anger log starts asking the question "Where were you when you got angry?" Answering this question will help you see the pattern of the settings in which you get angry. If you learn that you are usually angry when walking in the hallways, you can then ask why: Is it because someone is always ready to bully or tease you in the hallways (or you're worried they will be)? Or are you always losing your cool in English class because you did not get along with last year's English teacher and have "programmed" (taught) yourself to be angry with this year's teacher? What settings are especially difficult for you—places where you tend to be "set off" most often?

Encourage the class to identify their own anger settings. Record these under the heading "Settings" on the poster.

When you are using the anger log, say where you were when your anger got triggered. If you can notice where you are when you get angry, you can predict situations in which you need to be especially careful about managing your anger in a positive way.

ROLE-PLAY

Today we are going to learn how to *role-play*, or enact, an anger management situation. Who has a situation we could role-play where a physiological tool helped?

From the situations students volunteer, choose one that you think has good potential for illustrating the use of physiological tools. If students do not volunteer, you may go ahead and select a situation from the ones students discussed in the review or role-play the example involving Jonas and Steve.

Refer to your copy of "Procedures for Role-Playing" (Appendix A3), conduct the role-play accordingly, then use the following questions as a basis for stimulating discussion and dialogue. If you used the example involving Jonas and Steve, adapt the questions as needed.

To the main actor and coactors
1. What were you feeling as you role-played this situation?
2. When you are in a situation like this, where in your body do you feel your anger?

To the creator/director
3. How did the actors do role-playing your situation? Did they accurately portray your anger?
4. While you were in the actual situation, where in your body did you feel your anger?

To the main actor and coactors, then creator/director
Ask the actors a question or group of questions, then direct the same question(s) to the creator/director.

5. What tools did you decide to use?

6. Why did you decide to use the tools you did?

7. Did your tools work, or did you need different ones? (If you needed different tools, which ones?)

8. What happened inside your body when you interrupted your anger and used your tools instead?

9. How were your angry feelings different before and after you managed them?

To the observers

10. What did you think of the role-play? Did it seem realistic to you?

11. Did the tools you saw being used work, or do you think different tools would have been better? If so, which ones would you have used?

Make any summary comments you have about the role-play, then praise everyone generously for their contributions.

Closing

Today we practiced using some physiological tools by doing a role-play. We learned about anger triggers and that, although each trigger is unique to the individual, we have many triggers in common with other people. We also learned about anger settings and discovered that an awareness of our own anger-provoking places can be helpful. In fact, noticing our anger triggers and anger settings can contribute to help us stay in control.

Which physiological tools would you like to try out this week?

Acknowledge responses, then instruct students to circle those techniques on the new anger management logs. Instruct students to put their new anger log in their folders and collect (or have students save) their filled-out logs. Remind students where they can pick up copies of the new log and encourage them to use it whenever they experience anger-provoking situations, whether at school or at home.

Connecting Activity

Language Arts

Give each student a connecting activity handout. Briefly define *sage* (wise person) and *rage* (extremely angry), then review the instructions for the Sage or Rage puzzle as a group. Answer any questions students may have. Allow students to work alone or in small cooperative groups, or help the whole class work together to complete the puzzle.

Optional extension or homework: Have students make their own puzzles using at least four anger management–related words. You may find it helpful to visit a puzzle-making Website. Because Websites come and go, it is best to search for sites and check their "friendliness" before having students use them for this activity.

ANSWER KEY

1. Think
2. Cool
3. Relax
4. Positive

5. Ignore
6. Anger
7. Trigger

Connecting Activity

Name _____ Date _____

Complete this puzzle by using anger management words. Most have already been covered, but two have not. See if you can figure them out. If you get frustrated doing this, use one of the physiological tools we talked about to stay calm and in control.

SAGE OR RAGE

Down

1. Use your head to stay calm.

2. Another term for staying calm is keeping _____ .

3. A goal for our muscles.

5. A positive strategy we can use when someone is teasing us.

Across

4. When we handle our angry feelings without using violent behavior or language, we say the result is _____ .

6. A normal feeling.

7. The name we use for a situation that sets us off.

ANGER TRIGGERS AND SETTINGS

Anger Log 2

Name _____ Date _____

What was your trigger?

❏ Somebody started fighting with me.   ❏ Somebody took something of mine.

❏ Somebody teased me.   ❏ Somebody did something I didn't like.

❏ Somebody insisted I do something.   ❏ Other _____

Where were you when you got angry?

❏ School   ❏ Neighborhood   ❏ Home   ❏ Other _____

How angry were you?	1 not angry	2 mildly angry	3 moderately angry	4 really angry	5 burning mad

		How did you handle your anger?	**How will you handle your anger next time?**
Inappropriate responses	Yelling	❏	❏
	Throwing something	❏	❏
	Cursing	❏	❏
	Threatening someone	❏	❏
	Breaking something	❏	❏
	Hitting someone	❏	❏
	Other _____	❏	❏
Appropriate responses			
Physiological tools	Counting to 10, 20, 30	❏	❏
	Taking deep breaths	❏	❏
	Relaxing my muscles	❏	❏
	Other _____	❏	❏

ANGER TRIGGERS AND SETTINGS

Review

Name _____ Date _____

1. **Anger triggers and settings**

   An anger *trigger* is something that sets you off.

   An anger *setting* is a place where your anger is triggered.

2. **Triggers list.** Our class listed the following anger triggers.

   _____

   _____

   _____

   _____

   _____

3. **Anger settings.** Our class listed the following settings as places they tend to become angry.

   _____

   _____

   _____

   _____

   _____

4. **Role-play.** We role-played a situation that showed the use of physiological tool(s).

   Created/directed by _____

   Acted by _____

   Situation

   _____

   _____

   _____

   _____

   _____

   _____

   _____

   _____

5. **Anger log.** From this session on, the anger log includes space for you to track your anger triggers, anger settings, and use of physiological anger management tools.

6. **Other comments**

   _____

   _____

   _____

ANGER TRIGGERS AND SETTINGS

Leader Checklist

Leader name _____ Date of session _____

I covered the following topics today (*check all that apply*).

1. Review

   ❏ Reviewed physiological signs of anger.

   ❏ Made sure students know where to find and how to use the anger log.

   ❏ Checked for student use of the anger log to monitor their use of physiological techniques.

2. Introduction to triggers and settings

   ❏ Defined and generated a list of anger triggers.

   ❏ Defined and generated a list of anger settings.

3. Anger log

   ❏ Explained how to use the section for recording anger triggers.

   ❏ Explained how to use the section for recording settings in which anger occurs.

   ❏ Encouraged students to continue using their anger logs.

4. Role-play

   ❏ Helped students role-play a situation, using an example from the session.

   ❏ Used the role-play to clarify the use of physiologically based anger management techniques.

5. I also covered the following area(s).

   _____

   _____

   _____

Degrees of Anger/Other Anger Management Tools

Goals

▷ To introduce students to the idea that degrees of anger arousal vary, often according to specific variables

▷ To introduce additional techniques for managing anger

▷ To encourage students to reduce the level of anger arousal by substituting calming thoughts and behaviors

Objectives

▷ Continuing to identify angry feelings and the triggers and settings associated with them

▷ Identifying the degree of anger experienced in certain situations

▷ Learning that situations can be classified by whether an action is accidental or deliberate; one's familiarity with and feelings about the person(s) involved; and one's ability to decipher ("read") others' motives

▷ Expanding the *In Control* repertoire by learning that, in addition to physiological techniques, thinking and behavioral techniques are useful tools to manage anger

▷ Through role-playing, practicing ways to interrupt episodes of anger arousal and substitute calming thoughts and behaviors

Materials

▷ Easel pad (or another whole-class format)

▷ Student anger management folders

▷ Triggers and settings poster (from the previous session)

▷ Session 3 review sheet (one per student)

▷ Anger Log 3 (one per student)

▷ Connecting activity

Handout (one per student)

Markers or colored pencils

Overview

By this session, the students are usually involved in the anger management program. You can expect a core group to be active participants and the majority of the students to participate with a little encouragement. Students are usually eager to be involved in role-playing a recent incident. Depending on the class, the students may be ready to divide into small cooperative groups to develop and practice role-playing scenes. If so, you can then have the groups share and discuss their role-plays.

Once students begin volunteering situations on a regular basis, they will likely offer incidents in which they used an anger management technique other than a physiological one. In addition to a five-point anger arousal rating scale, the anger log introduces two new categories: thinking tools and behavioral tools. Session 6 expands on these new categories.

Leader Script

Review

Greet the students warmly. Distribute the Session 3 review sheet, prepared in advance, then discuss. Have students take turns reading parts of the review sheet aloud.

Did it help you to use your anger log to identify your anger triggers? How many of you used the log without being reminded?

Pause for a show of hands after each question.

As a result of your experiences since the last session, can we add any additional anger triggers to our list?

Pause for responses, recording them on the anger triggers and settings poster you began last session.

Now, what about where you were when you got angry? Let's list all the different settings you noticed.

Add student responses to the triggers and settings poster.

Did anyone use a physiological tool (taking deep breaths, counting, muscle relaxation) since the last session? Did you remember to record these on the log?

Pause for a show of hands after each question.

You will probably discover that you need to work very hard to use effective techniques to manage your anger when you are at number 5 ("burning mad").

Thinking and behavioral tools are new ways to help you stay in control.

Many different tools are available to help us manage our anger and stay in control. We have already discussed physiological tools. Today we are going to discuss thinking and behavioral tools. As long as we are in touch with our responses—bodily, thinking, behavioral—when we are angry, we can draw upon these parts of ourselves to stay in control.

It is really neat that all of the tools we are exploring are always with us, that we carry them with us at all times. Just as we use a needle and thread for one job and a wrench and a hammer for another, we will discover that we'll probably use more than one anger management tool to accomplish our "in control" tasks.

Your anger log now also includes two new anger management tools—thinking tools and behavioral tools. You can use these anger management tools, in addition to physiological tools, to keep from getting to numbers 4 or 5 on the anger scale or to bring yourself down if you get there. We will talk more in Session 6 about these new tools, but for the time being, let's get a feel for them by looking at some examples.

> *Refer students to the new anger log material. Briefly explain each type of anger management tool, working toward the following definitions. As you discuss, ask students for examples of times they used (or might have used) these new tools.*

Thinking tools

A thinking tool helps us substitute positive thoughts and feelings for angry ones. A main thinking tool is *self-talk*. Self-talk is the silent way you talk to yourself inside your head. *(Adapt as needed.)* For example, Jonas might tell himself, "There is so much more to me than my height. I am going to ignore Steve's insults." As Jonas has, in anger management we learn to use our thinking to coach ourselves to stay calm and in control. Usually we find that our thinking has an impact on our physiology, and vice versa.

> *Illustrate this point by saying the following, showing anger arousal by raising your voice, clenching your fists (really ham it up!): "Jacki bumped into me. She doesn't like me. She did it on purpose. I hate Jacki."*

What did you observe as I became more and more aroused by my thinking?

> *Answer: "You became more out of control and looked more and more angry." Next demonstrate the opposite: "Jacki bumped into me. She doesn't like me. Oh, well. I have many other friends. I'll just ignore her."*

What did you notice this time about my face? My body? My thinking?

Answer: "You stayed in control. You didn't look angry."

Good work, class. Now, a *self-statement* is a special type of self-talk in which we develop a personal slogan that we find is effective in assisting us to stay calm and in control—for example, "Keep cool" and "Ignore it." Let's list some more.

Write down students' ideas as they offer them: "I'm in control," "Chill out," "Relax," "Stay calm," "Keep it down."

Behavioral tools

A behavioral tool is a socially appropriate action we take to redirect ourselves when we are angry so that we stay in control. Examples include walking away, ignoring the situation, going for a run, and talking your problem out with a trusted friend or adult.

ROLE-PLAY

Let's create and enact a role-play in which you identify a trigger and a setting, then use one or more of the anger management tools you have learned to stay in control. After this role-play, we'll look at what using these tools did to the degree of anger. Who would like to share a situation for us to enact?

From the situations students volunteer, choose one that you think has good potential for illustrating degrees of anger. If students do not volunteer, you may select a situation from the ones students discussed in the review or role-play the following example.

Min arrived in class with a new hairstyle. Victor told her she looked ugly. Min felt the anger in her body. Her stomach was in knots, her heart and head were pounding, and her hands started sweating. She decided her anger was a "4" (really angry) on the anger scale. To keep from getting angrier, she *(Let students choose one):* (a) took three deep breaths, (b) counted to 10, or (c) relaxed her muscles. Then she reminded herself that it is important to make your own decisions about your appearance, no matter what anyone else says. Finally, she walked away.

Refer to your copy of "Procedures for Role-Playing" (Appendix A3), conduct the role-play accordingly, then ask the following questions. If you used Min's situation, adapt the questions as needed.

To the main actor

1. What were you feeling as you role-played this situation?

2. When you are in a situation like this, where in your body do you feel your anger?

To the creator/director

3. How did the actors do role-playing your situation? Did they accurately portray your anger?

4. While you were in the situation, where in your body did you feel your anger?

To the main actor and coactors, then creator/director

Ask the actors a question or group of questions, then direct the same question(s) to the creator/director.

5. Was the event accidental or deliberate?

6. What tools did you decide to use?

7. Why did you choose to use the tools you did?

8. Did your tools work, or did you need to use different ones? (If you needed different tools, which ones?)

9. What happened inside your body when you interrupted your anger and used your tools instead?

10. On our degrees of anger scale, how angry were you at first (with 1 being the least angry, and 5 the most)?

11. How were your angry feelings different before and after you managed them?

To the observers

12. What did you think of the role-play? Did it seem realistic to you?

13. Do you think the event was accidental or deliberate?

14. Did the tools you saw being used work, or do you think different tools would have been better? If so, which ones would you have used?

15. Do you think using these anger management tools would have an effect on your degree of anger? If so, what?

Make any summary comments you have about the role-play, then praise everyone generously for their contributions.

Closing

Today the session was about knowing your degree of anger arousal, or just how angry you are, then using this knowledge and some new anger management tools to stay at the low end of the anger scale. We discussed two new anger management tools: thinking tools and behavioral tools. We'll look closer at these tools in Session 6.

Collect students' filled-out anger logs, or have students save them in their anger management folders along with the review sheet for Session 3. Tell them where they can pick up copies of the new anger log, and encourage them to continue using it. Remind them to focus on their degree of anger and use of anger management tools, especially the new ones.

Connecting Activity

Visual Art

Give one connecting activity handout to each student. Review the instructions as a group. Answer any questions students may have. The activity calls for students to draw a cartoon. If students prefer, they may write the situation as a straight narrative.

Connecting Activity

Name _____ Date _____

Make up your own anger management situation and use the boxes given to draw a cartoon about it. Be sure that your main character uses a calming technique based on the physiology of anger. He or she may also use a thinking tool or a behavioral tool. Show how your main character reduces the degree of anger by *interrupting* angry responses and thoughts and by *substituting* "in control" responses and calm thoughts.

Anger Log 3

Name _____ Date _____

What was your trigger?

❏ Somebody started fighting with me.　　❏ Somebody took something of mine.

❏ Somebody teased me.　　　　　　　　❏ Somebody did something I didn't like.

❏ Somebody insisted I do something.　　❏ Other _____

Where were you when you got angry?

❏ School　❏ Neighborhood　❏ Home　❏ Other _____

How angry were you?	1 not angry	2 mildly angry	3 moderately angry	4 really angry	5 burning mad

		How did you handle your anger?	**How will you handle your anger next time?**
Inappropriate responses	Yelling	❏	❏
	Throwing something	❏	❏
	Cursing	❏	❏
	Threatening someone	❏	❏
	Breaking something	❏	❏
	Hitting someone	❏	❏
	Other _____	❏	❏
Appropriate responses			
Physiological tools	Counting to 10, 20, 30	❏	❏
	Taking deep breaths	❏	❏
	Relaxing my muscles	❏	❏
	Other _____	❏	❏
Thinking tools	Using self-talk/self-statement	❏	❏

Write down what you thought or said to yourself.

_____

_____

Behavioral tools	Talking it out	❏	❏
	Ignoring it	❏	❏
	Going for a run	❏	❏
	Walking away	❏	❏
	Other _____	❏	❏

Review

Name _____ Date _____

1. **Anger triggers and settings.** Our class added the following triggers and settings to the poster.

   Triggers

   _____

   _____

   Settings

   _____

   _____

2. **Degrees of anger arousal.** A person can get more or less angry, depending on the factors involved in the situation.

   You will probably react with less anger if someone bumps into you accidentally (by chance) than if someone bumps into you deliberately (on purpose).

   You will probably react with less anger to people you know and/or like as opposed to people you don't know and/or don't like.

   You will probably react with less anger when you are able to "read" other people's motives, or reasons for doing or not doing something.

3. **Anger log.** We added a five-point scale to help you determine how angry you get during a specific incident.

1	2	3	4	5
not angry	mildly angry	moderately angry	really angry	burning mad

   We also added and discussed two new anger management tools: thinking tools and behavioral tools. We learned about *self-talk* (a kind of thinking tool) and *self-statements* (short reminders to stay calm and in control).

4. **Role-play.** Our class role-played the following situation.

   Created/directed by _____

   Acted by _____

   Situation

   _____

   _____

   _____

   _____

   _____

   _____

   _____

   _____

   _____

   _____

Review, page 1 of 2

5. Other comments

_____

_____

_____

Leader Checklist

Leader name _____ Date of session _____

I covered the following topics today *(check all that apply)*.

1. Review

   ❏ Reviewed definitions of *trigger* and *setting*.

   ❏ Discussed student use of anger logs since the last session, especially in regard to recording triggers and settings.

   ❏ Reviewed and added anger triggers and settings to poster.

   ❏ Discussed student use of physiological techniques since the last session.

2. Degrees of anger arousal

   ❏ Defined terms related to anger arousal.

   ❏ Discussed factors that affect degree of anger arousal.

   Whether an event is accidental or deliberate

   Whether or not we know and like a person

   How well we "read" the other person's motives

3. Anger log

   ❏ Explained how to rate degrees of anger arousal using the five-point scale added to the log.

   ❏ Introduced thinking and behavioral anger management tools.

   ❏ Encouraged students to continue to use their anger management logs.

4. Role-play

   ❏ Helped students role-play a situation, using an example from the session.

   ❏ Used a physiological tool as well as thinking and/or behavioral tools.

   ❏ Stressed the effect of using these tools on degree of anger.

5. I also covered the following area(s):

   _____

   _____

   _____

Anger Management Criteria/ Self-Evaluation

Goals

▷ To help students learn the criteria for good anger management

▷ To help students begin to evaluate for themselves whether or not improvements are needed

▷ To give students the opportunity to continue practicing the use of anger management techniques in a role-play situation

Objectives

▷ Learning and applying specific criteria for good anger management to develop skills for self-evaluation

▷ Role-playing an anger management situation with the purpose of determining whether or not it meets the criteria for good anger management

▷ Learning that self-evaluation can suggest directions for improving anger management and strengthen feelings of self-competence

Materials

▷ Easel pad (or another whole-class format)

▷ Student anger management folders

▷ Triggers and settings poster (from the previous session)

▷ Session 4 review sheet (one per student)

▷ Anger Log 4 (one per student)

Overview

Learning to evaluate one's own actions, attitudes, and competence is a complex and advanced—yet invaluable—life skill. For many students, this session will be their first opportunity to develop the tool and habit of self-evaluation. It can be quite empowering for students to know they can decide on their own whether or not they handled anger well. This is an integral part of being in control.

Some students may be resistant to the self-evaluation process because they may perceive it as criticism. You can help them overcome these feelings and move toward more mature, helpful responses by being sensitive to such reactions. You can let the students know that growing up involves learning to balance self-acceptance and the need for self-improvement. Make the point that we all need to learn to be as tolerant of our own imperfections as we are of the imperfections of others. Model gentle criticism of the self as well as others.

Leader Script

Review

Greet the students warmly. Distribute the Session 4 review sheet, prepared in advance. Have students take turns reading the parts of the review sheet aloud. Discuss as a group. Remind them to keep the review sheets in their anger management folders.

Did using your anger logs help you in any way during the time since our last session? How many of you feel you used the log independently, without reminders?

Pause for a show of hands for each question.

Look at your anger logs and think about the time since we last met. Did anyone use any physiological tools? What about thinking tools? Behavioral tools?

Record students' names, situations, and tool used/type of tool. If a student mentions using a self-statement, record that as well.

Let's also look at how angry you were according to the 5-point degrees of anger scale, which we added last time to the log.

Have the students who volunteered situations rate how angry they were at the beginning and end of their situations. Record these numbers as well. For example:

Name	Situation	Tool/type	Before	After
Gabe	teacher gave low grade	deep breathing/physiological	4	2
Anton	insulted about family	self-talk/thinking ("Dial down.")	5	3
Layla	got called a "nerd"	ignored/behavioral	3	1

Next refer students to the anger triggers and situations poster.

Does anyone have any additional anger triggers to add to our ongoing list? What new settings could we add?

Record responses to each question as students give them. Encourage students to keep their review sheets in their folders. Remind them that at the end of the program they will have a summary of what the class worked on that will be useful for future reference.

Session Content

Anger management criteria can help you decide whether or not you are making your anger work for you.

During this session, we are going to discuss the *criteria* for good anger management, or how exactly you can judge how well you've used your anger management tools. The process of judging this for yourself is called *self-evaluation*. Who can give me a quick example of a situation in which you handled your anger well? How did you know you did a good job?

Have a few students briefly describe situations; acknowledge their comments on how they evaluated their response.

Criteria for good anger management

Basically, there are three ways you can tell whether or not you have managed your anger successfully. What do you think these might be?

Elicit and record the following criteria.

Staying in control

If you start yelling at someone, is that staying in control? *(Students respond.)* What could you do that would be staying in control?

Sample answers: "Stop and relax your muscles," "Walk away," "Talk calmly to the person."

Respecting people and property

What does it mean to respect people and property?

Sample answers: "Staying out of someone's face," "Not hitting," "Not throwing or breaking stuff," "Giving something you borrow back in as good a shape as you borrowed it."

Getting positive results

Most of the time, if you use good anger management skills, the result will be positive. That means the problem gets worked out and everyone's point of view is respected. However, even if you use your anger management tools perfectly, sometimes things just don't work out the way you'd like them to.

There are many things we can't control. Maybe someone is just a difficult person, or maybe he or she needs more practice with the anger management tools. Mostly, what we can control is ourselves.

At this point you may ask students to mention some situations in which they thought they handled themselves well but things didn't work out. Keep these mentions very brief and general to avoid having the discussion turn into a gripe session. Ask students if it helps to know they were in control and handled themselves well, even if things didn't work out. If someone answers no, reply that it would make a difference to you in that situation because you feel best about yourself when you are in control. Go on to explain the following.

Even though good anger management won't always result in a positive outcome right away, it can have a positive effect later on. For one thing, you're getting more practice yourself, and if you stay calm and in control this time, maybe the other person will rethink his or her position—or maybe not. Life isn't fair, but that doesn't mean you don't have a responsibility to keep yourself in control or that you should stop trying. Good anger management means you release your anger in acceptable ways, by using your anger management tools. When you do this, you deserve a big pat on the back and a round of applause. It's a hard goal to reach!

Signs of anger mismanagement

Anger mismanagement means you did not handle a situation as well as you might have. What do you think are some ways you can tell you are mismanaging your anger?

Pause for responses. Elicit and record the following criteria.

Losing control

Hurting people or damaging property

Getting negative results

Basically, these signs are the opposite of the criteria for good anger management. If you have mismanaged your anger, you didn't make your anger work for you. Don't feel bad or defensive, though. Learning to manage your anger requires a lot of practice!

Self-evaluation helps you decide for yourself whether or not you need more practice.

Distribute copies of Anger Log 4 and direct students to the new material.

Here's the newest version of the anger log. The log now includes a section to help you with self-evaluation. You check yes if you met the criteria for good anger management. You check no if you did not meet these criteria. If you check no, it probably means you need to think about what you could do differently next time to get better results, then keep on practicing.

ROLE-PLAY

Does anyone have a situation we could role-play where you used anger management tools, but maybe you didn't use the right tools, or you could have done better using the ones you did use? In other words, even though you tried, things didn't come out exactly as you wanted them to?

From the situations students volunteer, choose one that you think has good potential for illustrating use of anger management criteria. If students do not volunteer, you may select a situation from the ones they discussed in the review, or role-play the following example.

Harry was guarding Andy during the basketball game. Harry grabbed Andy by the arm, but the referee was not around to call a foul. Andy got angry and felt like knocking Harry to the floor. He felt his face flush and the muscles in his arms and shoulders tense. He knew he didn't want to lose control, so he tried to relax and "shake it off." In fact, he shook his hands and arms at his side. That helped Andy control his anger enough to keep his hands off Harry. Andy really got in Harry's face, though, and the things he said were pretty bad, bad enough for the referee who overheard him to give his team a technical foul.

Refer to your copy of "Procedures for Role-Playing" (Appendix A3), conduct the role-play accordingly, then ask the following questions as a basis for stimulating discussion and dialogue. If you used the example, adapt the questions as needed.

To the main actor and coactors

1. What were you feeling as you role-played this situation?

2. When you are in a situation like this, where in your body do you feel your anger?

To the creator/director

3. How did the actors do role-playing your situation? Did they accurately portray your anger?

4. While you were in the actual situation, where in your body did you feel your anger?

To the main actor and coactors, then creator/director

Ask the actors a question or group of questions, then direct the same question(s) to the creator/director.

5. Was the event accidental or deliberate?

6. What tools did you decide to use?

7. Why did you decide to use the tools you did?

8. Did your tools work, or did you need different ones? (If you needed different tools, which ones?)

9. On our degrees of anger scale, how angry were you at first (with 1 being the least angry, and 5 the most)?

10. How well did you meet the criteria for anger management? (Did you stay in control, respect people and property, and get positive results?)

11. What could you have done better?

   If the role-play showed anger mismanagement, this is a good place for the actors to perform a second role-play illustrating good anger management.

12. How were your angry feelings different before and after you managed them?

To the observers

13. What did you think of the role-play? Did it seem realistic to you?

14. Do you think the event was accidental or deliberate?

15. Did the tools you saw being used work, or do you think different tools would have been better? If so, which ones would you have used?

16. Do you think using these or other anger management tools would have an effect on your degree of anger? If so, what?

17. What do you think might have been done better to meet the criteria for good anger management?

   Make any summary comments you have about the role-play, then praise everyone generously for their contributions.

Closing

So far, we have talked about many tools you can use to stay in control of your anger and make it work for you. It's up to you to know how your body shows anger, recognize your own anger triggers and settings, and choose the anger management tools that will work best for you. This session has focused on criteria for self-evaluation—for judging how well you do so you'll know whether you are making your anger work for you or whether you need more practice. At the next session, we'll talk some more about how thinking and behavioral tools can help you stay calm and in control.

Collect students' filled-out anger logs, or have students save them in their anger management folders along with the review sheet for Session 4. Remind them where they can pick up copies of the new anger log, and encourage them to continue using it.

Connecting Activity

Current Events/Civics

Using the easel pad or another whole-class format, draw two columns. Label one plus (+) and one minus (–). Say, "Let's think about some current events in the news and applying our criteria for good anger management." As students describe events, ask them whether they belong in the plus column (met criteria) or the minus column (did not meet criteria).

Any daily newspaper will likely have stories that fall into each category. Here are some examples.

> *Examples of good anger management:* A person who was robbed testifies in court; people concerned with police violence plan a nonviolent march down Main Street; a school superintendent quits after the mayor cuts the budget; a basketball star who is called out of play goes to the bench.

> *Examples of anger mismanagement:* Teens are involved in a street fight; a mother beats her 3-year-old daughter; an unknown person breaks all the church windows.

Anger Log 4

Name _____ Date _____

What was your trigger?

❏ Somebody started fighting with me. ❏ Somebody took something of mine.

❏ Somebody teased me. ❏ Somebody did something I didn't like.

❏ Somebody insisted I do something. ❏ Other _____

Where were you when you got angry?

❏ School ❏ Neighborhood ❏ Home ❏ Other _____

How angry were you?

1	2	3	4	5
not angry	mildly angry	moderately angry	really angry	burning mad

		How did you handle your anger?	How will you handle your anger next time?
Inappropriate responses	Yelling	❏	❏
	Throwing something	❏	❏
	Cursing	❏	❏
	Threatening someone	❏	❏
	Breaking something	❏	❏
	Hitting someone	❏	❏
	Other _____	❏	❏
Appropriate responses			
Physiological tools	Counting to 10, 20, 30	❏	❏
	Taking deep breaths	❏	❏
	Relaxing my muscles	❏	❏
	Other _____	❏	❏
Thinking tools	Using self-talk/self-statement	❏	❏

Write down what you thought or said to yourself.

_____

_____

Behavioral tools	Talking it out	❏	❏
	Ignoring it	❏	❏
	Going for a run	❏	❏
	Walking away	❏	❏
	Other _____	❏	❏

Did you make your anger work for you?

❏ Yes   I stayed in control, respected people and property, and had positive results.

❏ No   I lost control, hurt people or property, and/or had negative results.

SESSION 5

66

ANGER MANAGEMENT CRITERIA/SELF-EVALUATION

Review

Name _____ Date _____

1. **Anger triggers and settings.** Our class added the following triggers and settings to the list.

   Triggers

   _____

   _____

   Settings

   _____

   _____

2. **Anger management tools/types and anger ratings**

			Anger rating	
Name	*Situation*	*Tool/type*	*Before*	*After*

3. **Anger management criteria**

Good anger management	*Anger mismanagement*
Staying in control	Losing control
Respecting people and property	Hurting people or property
Getting positive results	Getting negative results

   Do negative results always mean you mismanaged your anger? Our class said:

   _____

   _____

4. **Anger log.** We added a self-evaluation section to the anger log, listing criteria to help you judge for yourself how well you manage your anger. Having this information will help you decide whether you need to think about ways to get better results next time or practice more.

5. **Role-play.** We role-played a situation and then applied anger management criteria to it.

Created/directed by _____

Acted by _____

Situation

_____

_____

_____

_____

_____

_____

_____

_____

_____

_____

_____

6. **Other comments**

_____

_____

_____

ANGER MANAGEMENT CRITERIA/SELF-EVALUATION

Leader Checklist

Leader name _____ Date of session _____

I covered the following topics today *(check all that apply)*.

1. Review
   - ❑ Discussed student use of anger logs since the last session, especially with regard to identifying triggers and settings and determining degree of anger.
   - ❑ Discussed student use of anger management tools since the last session.

2. Anger triggers and settings, tools/types, and anger ratings
   - ❑ Added items to the anger triggers and settings poster.
   - ❑ Asked students to identify anger management tools and types.
   - ❑ Asked students to rate degree of anger.

3. Evaluation criteria
   - ❑ Defined criteria that indicate good anger management: staying in control, respecting people and property, getting positive results.
   - ❑ Defined criteria that indicate anger mismanagement: losing control, hurting people or property, getting negative results.
   - ❑ Explained that, even if a person tries hard and does a good job of using the tools, results might not be positive.

4. Anger log
   - ❑ Added a self-evaluation component to the anger log.
   - ❑ Encouraged students to continue using their anger logs.

5. Role-play
   - ❑ Helped students role-play a situation, using an example from the session.
   - ❑ Encouraged students to apply anger management criteria to the role-play situation.

6. I also covered the following area(s).

   _____

   _____

   _____

Thinking and Behavioral Tools

Goals

▷ To teach students the cognitively based anger management techniques of self-talk and self-statements

▷ To give students more detailed information about behavioral tools and their use

Objectives

▷ Learning that thinking tools are an important part of good anger management

▷ Understanding that self-talk and self-statements can help one calm down and stay in control

▷ Consolidating knowledge about thinking and behavioral tools through role-playing

Materials

▷ Easel pad (or another whole-class format)

▷ Student anger management folders

▷ Anger settings and triggers poster (from the previous session)

▷ Session 5 review sheet (one per student)

▷ Anger Log 5 (one per student)

▷ Connecting activity

   Handout (one per student)

   Markers or colored pencils

Overview

This session expands on the brief introduction to thinking and behavioral tools presented in Session 4. In describing cognitively based techniques, you can help students identify an aspect of their experience they previously may not have considered—the fact that what they think has a profound influence on what they feel and consequently do. The thinking tools are *self-talk* (the general way people think to themselves about a situation, other people, or even themselves) and *self-statements* (words or phrases that serve as a reminder to think and behave in a positive way—specifically, to cool down and/or use an anger management tool). It is important to note that the concept of using one's thoughts to manage anger will be new to many students, as will the idea that self-talk can be positive or negative.

Behavioral tools are defined in the session as something you *do* to deal with your anger, before, during, or after a difficult situation—for example, walking away, ignoring, going for a run or working out, or talking the situation over with a trusted friend or adult.

Students are usually able to create, direct, and act out role-plays with little assistance by this point in the program. In fact, they will probably now be in the habit of "saving up" incidents to process during the next anger management session.

Leader Script

Review

Greet the students warmly. Distribute the Session 5 review sheet, which you have prepared in advance. Have students take turns reading the parts of the review sheet aloud. Discuss.

Who has an example of good anger management recorded on his or her anger log? That means a situation in which you met the criteria of staying in control, respecting people and property, and—at least most of the time—getting a positive result.

Encourage brief discussion of situations that met (and did not meet) these criteria.

It looks as though many of you are really using your anger management tools to help you stay in control. Would someone please remind us what tools we've already discussed and practiced?

Pause for responses. Elicit a few examples of physiological, thinking, and behavioral tools.

Does anyone have any additional anger triggers to add to our ongoing list? What new settings could we add?

Record responses to each question as students give them.

Session Content

In Session 4, we talked briefly about thinking and behavioral anger management tools. Some of you may have used these tools already. Today we'll go into more detail about them.

Thinking tools can help you make your anger work for you.

Just as knowing about your physiology helps you manage your anger, knowing what you are saying to yourself—in other words, thinking—can also help you stay calm and in control.

The two main thinking tools are self-talk and self-statements. *Self-talk* is what you think to yourself about something someone does or something that happens. Self-talk can either help you or hurt you, depending on what kind it is. Here's an example:

> Leann's family doesn't have a lot of money, so she can't afford to wear designer clothes. Another girl in Leann's class, Kendra, has been hassling her by saying the clothes she wears make her look like a loser. Leann might say to herself, "Kendra is such a slob! She has no right to bug me about what I choose to wear. I'll show her!"

Do you think that kind of self-talk would help Leann stay calm and manage her anger in a positive way? *(Students respond.)* What effect do you suppose using that kind of self-talk would have on Leann?

> *Sample answers: "It would get Leann all worked up," "Her anger would be getting stronger and stronger," "Her adrenaline would be pumping, and she'd be ready to fight it out."*

When a situation intensifies, we say it has *escalated*, in the way an escalator goes up. In fact, this kind of self-talk is very negative.

Positive and negative self-talk have very different effects.

Suppose you are baby-sitting a young child. For some reason, the child becomes upset, out of control, and angry. What would you say to the child to help him or her calm down?

> *Sample answers: "Take some deep breaths," "Don't worry, you'll be fine," "Let's find something you like to do," "Your mom will be home soon."*

What could Leann say to herself that would be positive and would help her stay calm and in control?

> *Sample answers: "It's no big deal—it's not what you wear that's important but what's inside," "Lots of other people think I dress fine," "It's sad that Kendra is*

so unhappy with herself that she has nothing better to do than bother other people."

As we've seen, sometimes you can use more than one anger management tool to help yourself stay calm until you can think clearly. Leann might take three deep breaths (a physiological tool) before walking away (a behavioral tool). If Leann told herself, "I can stay out of trouble by walking away," she would be using positive self-talk (a thinking tool).

The value of positive self-talk is that it helps you calm down so you can make choices that more carefully direct what you do. All of us can gain better control by saying or thinking things like this to ourselves.

A self-statement is a quick way to remind yourself to change your thinking.

Suppose in the situation with Leann, she stopped herself long enough to think, "I am pretty angry at Kendra, but I am not going to let her get to me." That would be a pretty long-winded way of reminding herself to stay in control. We call a shortened version of self-talk a *self-statement.* How could you shorten Leann's self-talk so it would be a self-statement?

> *Sample answer: "Walk away."*

A self-statement is a personal, special word or phrase you use to interrupt your angry, out-of-control state and redirect yourself toward a calmer, more in-control state. You could consider your self-statement a special kind of tool that helps you remember to calm down and use your other anger management tools.

Can you think of some more self-statements that might be helpful? Remember, self-statements should be short so they will be easy to remember.

> *Pause for responses, recording them as students speak; sample answers: "Ignore it," "Breathe," Stay calm," "Chill out," and the like.*

ROLE-PLAY

Let's try role-playing an anger management situation in two different ways. In the first way, someone uses negative self-talk and becomes even more angry and out of control. In the second, let's change the situation so the person uses positive self-talk to calm down and stay in control. Does anyone have a situation that shows how self-talk affects how you are feeling and behaving?

> *From the situations students volunteer, choose one that you think has good potential for illustrating the use of self-talk/self-statements. If students do not volunteer, select a situation from the ones students discussed in the review, or role-play Leann's situation or the following example. Adapt the questions as needed.*

Eduardo called Marlisa "ugly." Marlisa thought, "I'll get *him!*" Then she screeched, "You pig!" Eduardo shoved her, and the bus monitor gave them each a detention. Now they will have to sit together in the same room for an hour after school! (*Marlisa used negative self-talk.*)

Eduardo called Marlisa "ugly." Marlisa thought, "Ignore it." Then she turned and talked to her best friend about this Friday's party. Eduardo looked around for someone else to pick on. (*Marlisa used a positive self-statement.*)

Refer to your copy of "Procedures for Role-Playing" (Appendix A3), conduct the role-play accordingly, then ask the following questions as a basis for stimulating discussion and dialogue.

To the main actor and coactors

1. What were you feeling as you role-played this situation?

2. When you are in a situation like this, where in your body do you feel your anger?

To the creator/director

3. How did the actors do role-playing your situation? Did they accurately portray your anger?

4. While you were in the actual situation, where in your body did you feel your anger?

To the main actor and coactors, then creator/director

Ask the actors a question or group of questions, then direct the same question(s) to the creator/director.

5. Was the event accidental or deliberate?

6. What tools did you decide to use?

7. Why did you decide to use the tools you did?

8. Did your tools work, or did you need different ones? (If you needed different tools, which ones?)

9. On our degrees of anger scale, how angry were you at first (with 1 being the least angry, and 5 the most)?

10. How well did you meet the criteria for anger management? (Did you stay in control, respect people and property, and get positive results?)

11. What could you have done better?

    If the role-play showed anger mismanagement, this is a good place for the actors to perform a second role-play illustrating good anger management.

12. How were your angry feelings different before and after you managed them?

To the observers

13. What did you think of the role-play? Did it seem realistic to you?

14. Do you think the event was accidental or deliberate?

15. Did the tools you saw being used work, or do you think different tools would have been better? If so, which ones would you have used?

16. Do you think using these or other anger management tools would have an effect on your degree of anger? If so, what?

17. What do you think might have been done better to meet the criteria for good anger management?

Make any summary comments you have about the role-play, then praise everyone generously for their contributions.

Behavioral tools help you stay in control.

Another way to help yourself stay in control is to use a behavioral tool, alone or in combination with any of the other anger management tools. A behavioral tool is something you *do* to deal with your anger. For example, what did Marlisa say to herself in our example at the beginning of this session? And what did she do?

Pause for responses. If you used an original student role-play and not the situation involving Marlisa and Eduardo, adapt this material accordingly.

Marlisa used a self-statement ("Ignore it"), then she actually went ahead and ignored Eduardo. When she did that, she was using a behavioral tool. What are some examples of behavioral tools you could use to help you control your anger?

Pause for responses, recording them as students speak. (Anger Log 5 lists talk it out, ignore it, go for a run, walk away.) Briefly discuss the circumstances relating to the behavioral tools your class identifies. If students do not bring up "talk it out," introduce the following ideas yourself.

What about the behavioral tool "talk it out"? If you think you might find yourself in a tight spot, or you actually have, you could seek out someone with whom to discuss the situation, either before or after it happens. Let's name some people who might help by talking with you.

Record responses as students speak. Sample answers: a parent, another relative (e.g., aunt, grandfather), a teacher or school counselor, a friend, a religious leader.

Before a difficult situation, talking it out gives you time to think about what might happen and how you want to react. This will help you stay in control and handle the situation well. And if you talk it out after the situation, the other person can help you cool down and get a different perspective on how things went. Then you might be better able to stay cool before there's a problem next time.

If time permits, ask for volunteers to direct and act out a role-play to illustrate the use of a behavioral tool of the group's choice. Conduct the role-play according to the instructions in Appendix A3; follow up with specific questions as appropriate.

If you know all the anger management tools, you can choose the best ones for you.

Give each student a copy of Anger Log 5. Refer students to the section of the log on thinking and behavioral tools.

Here's the newest version of the log. Continue to use your physiological tools, but between now and our next meeting, pay special attention to how you use these other tools.

Closing

Today's session concerned the thinking tools, self-talk and self-statements, and focused on how negative and positive self-talk have very different effects on how you feel when you are angry. We also discussed behavioral tools, or things you can do before, during, or after you find yourself in a difficult situation—that is, one with potential anger triggers. In the next session, you'll receive the Final Anger Log and have a chance to develop an individual anger management plan based on the things you've learned so far.

Next direct students' attention to the blank lines under "Thinking tools" for filling in self-talk and self-statements.

As a homework assignment, before the next session I want you to develop some self-talk and a self-statement that you think will work for *you* when you are angry, write these ideas on the new anger log, and, if you have the chance, try them out. Your self-talk and self-statement don't need to work for anyone else, but they should be something that will help you interrupt your own angry state. Remember, self-statements should be short and easy to remember.

Collect students' filled-out anger logs, or have students save them in their anger management folders along with the review sheet for Session 5. Remind them where they can pick up copies of the new anger log, and encourage them to continue using it.

Connecting Activity

Language Arts/Visual Art

Give each student a connecting activity handout, and review the directions. Assign as an in-class activity or as homework.

Connecting Activity

Name _____ Date _____

Select a self-statement and a situation in which this self-statement will help you manage your anger. Write a story that shows how you have used or plan to use the self-statement. Make sure your story shows how angry you felt and how the self-statement helped you calm down and stay in control. If you like, you can also show how you used a behavioral tool.

Self-statement

_____

Story

_____

_____

_____

_____

_____

_____

_____

_____

_____

_____

_____

_____

_____

_____

_____

_____

_____

_____

_____

_____

THINKING AND BEHAVIORAL TOOLS

Anger Log 5

Name _____ Date _____

What was your trigger?

❏ Somebody started fighting with me. ❏ Somebody took something of mine.

❏ Somebody teased me. ❏ Somebody did something I didn't like.

❏ Somebody insisted I do something. ❏ Other _____

Where were you when you got angry?

❏ School ❏ Neighborhood ❏ Home ❏ Other _____

How angry were you?	1 not angry	2 mildly angry	3 moderately angry	4 really angry	5 burning mad

		How did you handle your anger?	How will you handle your anger next time?
Inappropriate responses	Yelling	❏	❏
	Throwing something	❏	❏
	Cursing	❏	❏
	Threatening someone	❏	❏
	Breaking something	❏	❏
	Hitting someone	❏	❏
	Other _____	❏	❏
Appropriate responses			
Physiological tools	Counting to 10, 20, 30	❏	❏
	Taking deep breaths	❏	❏
	Relaxing my muscles	❏	❏
	Other _____	❏	❏
Thinking tools	Using self-talk/self-statement	❏	❏

Write down what you thought or said to yourself.

_____

_____

Behavioral tools	Talking it out	❏	❏
	Ignoring it	❏	❏
	Going for a run	❏	❏
	Walking away	❏	❏
	Other _____	❏	❏

Did you make your anger work for you?

❏ Yes   I stayed in control, respected people and property, and had positive results.

❏ No   I lost control, hurt people or property, and/or had negative results.

Review

Name _____ Date _____

1. **Anger triggers and settings.** Our class added the following triggers and settings to the poster.

   Triggers

   _____

   _____

   Settings

   _____

   _____

2. **Thinking tools.** *Self-talk* is what you think to yourself about something someone does or something that happens. Self-talk can be either positive or negative. A *self-statement* is a shortened version of your self-talk. We identified some possible self-statements.

   _____

   _____

   _____

3. **Behavioral tools.** A behavioral tool is something you do to deal with your anger. Our class identified these behavioral tools.

   _____

   _____

   _____

4. **Role-play.** We role-played a situation in which the main character showed how negative self-talk can make someone angrier and how using a positive self-statement can help a person calm down and stay in control.

   Created/directed by _____

   Acted by _____

   Situation

   _____

   _____

   _____

   _____

   _____

   _____

   _____

   _____

   _____

   _____

5. **Anger log.** The anger log stayed the same this time, but we added a space for you to fill in your own personal self-talk/self-statement.

6. **Other comments**

_____

_____

_____

THINKING AND BEHAVIORAL TOOLS

Leader Checklist

Leader name _____ Date of session _____

I covered the following topics today (*check all that apply*).

1. Review

   ❑ Discussed student use of anger logs since the last session, especially with regard to anger management criteria.

   ❑ Discussed student use of anger management tools since the last session.

   ❑ Reviewed and added new anger triggers and settings to the poster.

2. Thinking tools

   ❑ Defined *self-talk* and *self-statement*.

   ❑ Encouraged students to come up with their own self-statements.

   ❑ Discussed the different effects of positive and negative self-talk.

3. Role-play

   ❑ Helped students role-play a situation, using an example from the session.

   ❑ Role-played the situation two ways: first illustrating negative self-talk, next illustrating use of a positive self-statement.

4. Behavioral tools

   ❑ Explained that a behavioral tool is something you do to deal with your anger.

   ❑ Encouraged students to generate a number of examples of behavioral tools.

5. Anger log

   ❑ Added a space for students to write their own personal self-talk/self-statements.

   ❑ Encouraged students to continue using their anger logs.

6. I also covered the following area(s).

   _____

   _____

   _____

Final Anger Log/Individual Anger Management Plans

Goals

▷ To encourage student awareness of the most difficult anger management situations for individuals

▷ To give students the opportunity to role-play these situations in a safe, supportive atmosphere

▷ To guide students in developing an individualized anger management plan based on this self-knowledge

Objectives

▷ Becoming aware of personally difficult anger management situations

▷ Developing and illustrating, in a creative way, an individual anger management plan for dealing with these situations

▷ Understanding that each person's anger management plan is unique

Materials

▷ Easel pad (or another whole-class format)

▷ Student anger management folders

▷ Session 6 review sheet (one per student)

▷ Anger triggers and settings poster (from the last session)

▷ Final Anger Log (one per student)

▷ Ten Role-Play Questions (one per student)

▷ Poster board (one piece per student)

▷ Markers or colored pencils

▷ Connecting activity: Materials specified

Overview

In this session, the anger log is complete with the addition of a scale for self-rating the degree of success students experience in situations that call upon them to use their anger management tools. The overall rating helps students further develop self-evaluation skills.

This session also helps students develop an individualized anger management plan, illustrate it in a creative and vivid way, and share it with the class. Doing so conveys the idea that planning ahead is critical. Prior to creating these individual plans, however, students have an opportunity to role-play, preferably two situations. At this point, students are familiar with role-play procedures and have likely internalized much of the questioning process that follows role-playing. Before enacting the situations, they receive a handout entitled "Ten Role-Play Questions." This handout will be useful in this session, the remaining sessions, and in the first booster session, in which students conduct a role-play on their own.

By this time, students have developed a certain comfort level in thinking about and discussing anger management situations. As a result, the anger management situations that are raised may be more difficult ones. Extremely provocative situations that challenge the ability of these young teens (and almost-teens) to maintain self-control or situations of a more private nature may emerge. Be extra sensitive and vigilant when a youngster reveals information in class about his or her private life outside of school. Gently redirect the student if you think he or she may be on the verge of revealing something compromising or illegal—for example, that a parent is alcoholic or abusive, or that the parent or student has committed a crime. If information of this nature does slip out, continue to focus on the anger management issues, and in private offer immediate and appropriate assistance for the personal issues involved.

Following the role-plays, students think through and document their own individual anger management plans. The process of creating an individual plan offers an excellent opportunity to clarify important concepts presented thus far and to emphasize the differences among people's anger management plans. Stress that each student is an individual who needs to know his or her own pattern of anger arousal and who needs to develop his or her own tools and strategies for anger management. What works for one student may not work for another; each student needs to find the tools that help him or her the most.

Finally, although you may still find that some students will attempt to justify the use of physical force to solve problems—and may present some compelling arguments as to why they should do so—it is important to take a firm stand that there are always many other options.

Leader Script

Review

Greet the students warmly. Distribute the Session 6 review sheet, prepared before the session, and have individual students read the separate parts aloud. Discuss. Remind students to continue saving their review sheets in their anger management folders.

Did our discussion in the last session about thinking and behavioral tools help you when you used the anger log since the last session?

Pause briefly for a show of hands and comments.

Does anyone have any additional anger triggers to add to our ongoing list? What new settings could we add?

Record responses to each question on the anger triggers and settings poster.

Now let's make a list of the self-statements you came up with and recorded on your anger logs. Who would like to briefly share an experience in which you used a self-statement?

Record students' self-statements: "Chill," "Relax," "Move on," and so forth, then have a few students describe what happened when they put their statements to use.

I hope you will continue to experiment with finding self-statements that work for you. If you wish to make a small sign of your favorite self-statements for your desk or decorate your anger management folder with it as a reminder, please feel free to do so.

Session Content

Today, with the addition of one new section, the anger log is complete. We'll talk about the anger log, role-play some difficult anger management situations, and discuss why making an individual plan for tough anger management situations is important. Finally, you'll have a chance to make your own individualized anger management plan. Before we start, though, who can remind the class what the goal of good anger management is? How can you tell if you've used your anger management tools well?

Allow responses to these questions: The goal is to make your anger work for you instead of getting you in trouble. You can tell if you've done well by applying the criteria for good anger management (stay in control, respect people and property, get positive results).

The final anger log includes all aspects of anger management covered in this program.

As you know, each new anger management skill and tool you have learned has been added to the anger log, session by session. The final section of the log gives you a chance to record an overall rating of your own anger management performance.

Give each student a copy of the Final Anger Log. Direct students' attention to the last section on the log, "How did you handle the situation?"

From this point on, you can circle a number from 1 to 5 to rate how you think you did in managing your anger. Rating how you handle a situation can help you *analyze* your performance, or study and think about it in order to understand it better. Analyzing your performance can lead you to think about ways to improve your anger management in the future.

So far, you have identified your own anger triggers and settings, learned to tell the difference between deliberate and accidental provocations, and practiced using physiological, thinking, and behavioral tools. You've also made choices about which tools to use, based on what works best for you.

ROLE-PLAY

Right now, let's tackle a really tough anger management situation. Maybe someone has spread a terrible rumor about you, or your being passed on to the next grade hinges on whether or not you get a passing grade in a certain class. Maybe someone has threatened you with physical harm, or even assaulted you. Who could share a difficult situation like this for us to role-play?

From the situations students volunteer, choose one that you think is difficult but not too personal or emotionally charged. If students do not volunteer, you may select a situation from the ones students discussed in the review or role-play one of the following situations.

While Jarod was changing for football practice, Antoine walked by and slammed Jarod into his locker. Jarod was stunned. His left arm started hurting immediately. "That son of a bitch," he thought. I'm gonna kill him!" In a flash, Jarod took after Antoine. A movie of what would happen next ran in his mind: He would pummel Antoine. This image helped him interrupt his anger. "And what would that prove?" he asked himself. That he could be suspended and get in trouble with his football coach, that's what. He took three deep breaths and put the brakes on. "Antoine is not worth getting thrown off the team," he said to himself.

Sara got home an hour after her curfew. Her mother told her she was grounded and could not go to the basketball game on Friday. Sara told her mother she would go wherever she wanted to go. Her mother said, "Don't talk to me like that, young lady. Get to your room!" Sara wanted to tell her mother to go to hell, but she knew her mother meant business. She did go to her room. It was hard for her to cool off. She thought, "She is such a controlling bitch. I can take care of myself. I hate her!" She took some deep breaths and felt a little calmer. Then she thought, "Getting myself more and more worked up isn't going to solve anything. To her, I guess I'll always be her little girl. She probably just wants to make sure I'm safe."

Conduct the role-play according to the procedures described in Appendix A3. After the role-play, give each student a copy of the Ten Role-Play Questions.

We've done a lot of role-plays so far in this program, so you probably already know many of the questions we ask afterwards. Here's a list of the main ones. These don't always get asked in the same order, but please follow along to make sure we ask them all.

Refer to your copy of "Procedures for Role-Playing" (Appendix A3), conduct the role-play accordingly, then ask the following questions as a basis for stimulating discussion and dialogue.

To the main actor and coactors

1. What were you feeling as you role-played this situation?

2. When you are in a situation like this, where in your body do you feel your anger?

To the creator/director

3. How did the actors do role-playing your situation? Did they accurately portray your anger?

4. While you were in the actual situation, where in your body did you feel your anger?

To the main actor and coactors, then creator/director

Ask the actors a question or group of questions, then direct the same question(s) to the creator/director.

5. Was the event accidental or deliberate?

6. What tools did you decide to use?

7. Why did you decide to use the tools you did?

8. Did your tools work, or did you need different ones? (If you needed different tools, which ones?)

9. On our degrees of anger scale, how angry were you at first (with 1 being the least angry, and 5 the most)?

10. How well did you meet the criteria for anger management? (Did you stay in control, respect people and property, and get positive results?)

11. On our scale for overall rating, what number would you give yourself (with 1 being the poorest performance, and 5 being the best)?

12. What could you have done better?

If the role-play showed anger mismanagement, this is a good place for the actors to perform a second role-play illustrating good anger management.

13. How were your angry feelings different before and after you managed them?

To the observers

14. What did you think of the role-play? Did it seem realistic to you?

15. Do you think the event was accidental or deliberate?

16. Did the tools you saw being used work, or do you think different tools would have been better? If so, which ones would you have used?

17. Do you think using these or other anger management tools would have an effect on your degree of anger? If so, what?

18. What do you think might have been done better to meet the criteria for good anger management?

19. Do you think the overall ratings we discussed are accurate? If not, what ratings would you assign and why?

> *Make any summary comments you have about the role-play, then praise everyone generously for their contributions.*

Making an individual plan helps you manage your anger better.

Now that we've role-played a couple of difficult situations, let's think about individual anger management plans: In order to make a good plan, you need to know in advance what your personal anger triggers and settings are, how angry you may get, and what tools will really help *you* interrupt your state of anger arousal so you can stay calm and in control while meeting your needs and still respecting others' needs.

> *At this point, you may use the situations you role-played as spin-offs to devise an individual anger management plan, or you may use the following hypothetical situation.*

Let's try making an anger management plan for Ramon, who has to deal with the same situation every day: Each morning at the bus stop, a kid in the next grade calls Ramon's mother names. The kid has even pushed Ramon down a couple of times. What plan could Ramon make to help him make his anger work for him?

> *Talk through the planning process for the situation, taking students' suggestions and helping them build a thoughtful plan, including any or all of the information covered by the anger log to this point.*

What if Ramon wanted to make a poster of his individual anger management plan to help him remember it? What do you think he might want to include in his poster?

> *Ramon's poster included a concise description of the problem, degree of anger, useful anger management tools, and outcome—and turned out in the form of a poem.*

Push me down?

Burning mad!

Say "I'm OK,"

That's *my* way.

In this school,

I'm too cool!

Give each student a piece of poster board and markers or colored pencils. Ask students to write words or phrases (a brief poem or rap if they wish) to show their own anger management situation and plan. Encourage them to decorate their posters however they wish, and give lots of encouragement! Leave time for students to share their posters with the class. When they do, stress how different the plans are—how everyone has his or her own unique way of managing anger.

Closing

This session focused on creating and illustrating an individual anger management plan for a situation you feel is really a problem for you, and everyone's plan was different. You plan ahead for problem situations for the same reason the school has fire drills: You don't want to have to stop and think when the fire starts! As of this session, the anger log is complete—this is the version you will use in the future.

Share what general anger management improvements you (and other staff, if appropriate) have observed in the class. For example:

Some of you are using the log as a tool to help you avoid inappropriate behavior and stay in control. I'm seeing a lot more people fill out anger logs without being reminded. I am also pleased that more of you are willing to talk out problems and listen to one another before your anger escalates into fights. Keep up the good work!

Collect students' filled-out anger logs, or have students save them (and the Ten Role-Play Questions handout) in their anger management folders along with the review sheet for Session 6. Remind them where they can pick up copies of the Final Anger Log. Encourage students to carry out their individual plans at the next opportunity and to use the log to record their experiences.

Connecting Activity

Language Arts/Visual Art/Music/Dance

Encourage students to create more poems or raps, perhaps adding music or movement. If the equipment is available, students will enjoy making audiotapes or videotapes of the works they create. Students might also make and liberally illustrate a large mural of their individual plans, which everyone in the school could appreciate, or they might create a mini-play or dance.

Final Anger Log

Name _____ Date _____

What was your trigger?

- ❏ Somebody started fighting with me.
- ❏ Somebody teased me.
- ❏ Somebody insisted I do something.
- ❏ Somebody took something of mine.
- ❏ Somebody did something I didn't like.
- ❏ Other _____

Where were you when you got angry?

- ❏ School ❏ Neighborhood ❏ Home ❏ Other _____

How angry were you?

1	2	3	4	5
not angry	mildly angry	moderately angry	really angry	burning mad

		How did you handle your anger?	How will you handle your anger next time?
Inappropriate responses	Yelling	❏	❏
	Throwing something	❏	❏
	Cursing	❏	❏
	Threatening someone	❏	❏
	Breaking something	❏	❏
	Hitting someone	❏	❏
	Other _____	❏	❏
Appropriate responses			
Physiological tools	Counting to 10, 20, 30	❏	❏
	Taking deep breaths	❏	❏
	Relaxing my muscles	❏	❏
	Other _____	❏	❏
Thinking tools	Using self-talk/self-statement	❏	❏

Write down what you thought or said to yourself.

_____

_____

Behavioral tools	Talking it out	❏	❏
	Ignoring it	❏	❏
	Going for a run	❏	❏
	Walking away	❏	❏
	Other _____	❏	❏

Did you make your anger work for you?

- ❏ Yes I stayed in control, respected people and property, and had positive results.
- ❏ No I lost control, hurt people or property, and/or had negative results.

How did you handle the situation?

1	2	3	4	5
poorly	not so well	OK	well	great

Ten Role-Play Questions

Name _____ Date _____

1. What was your anger trigger? (What happened?)

2. What was the setting? (Where were you?)

3. Was the event accidental or deliberate?

4. How angry were you?

1	2	3	4	5
not angry	mildly angry	moderately angry	really angry	burning mad

5. Where in your body did you feel your anger?

6. What were you thinking when you were angry? (What self-talk/self-statements did you use?)

7. Did you have a plan for managing your anger? If so, what was it?

8. What tools did you use? Did they work, or did you need different tools? If so, which ones?

9. Did you meet the criteria for good anger management? (Did you stay in control, respect people and property, and get positive results?)

10. Overall, how do you think you handled the situation?

1	2	3	4	5
poorly	not so well	OK	well	great

Review

Name _____ Date _____

1. **Anger triggers and settings.** Our class added the following triggers and settings to the poster.

   Triggers

   _____
   _____

   Settings

   _____
   _____

2. **Final anger log.** The final anger log includes all aspects of anger management covered in the program. The final section of the log gives you a chance to record an overall rating of your own anger management performance, on a scale of 1 to 5.

3. **Role-play.** Our class role-played a difficult anger management situation, using the Ten Role-Play Questions as a guide for asking questions afterward.

   Created/directed by _____

   Acted by _____

   Situation

   _____
   _____
   _____
   _____
   _____
   _____
   _____
   _____
   _____
   _____
   _____
   _____

4. **Individual anger management plans.** As a group, our class came up with the following anger management plan for _____ .

   _____
   _____
   _____
   _____
   _____
   _____
   _____

5. **Anger management posters.** Our class created and shared anger management posters that illustrated our individual anger management plans.

6. **Other comments**

_____

_____

_____

Leader Checklist

Leader name _____ Date of session _____

I covered the following topics today (*check all that apply*).

1. Review

   ❏ Discussed student use of anger logs since the last session, especially with regard to self-statements.

   ❏ Discussed student use of anger management tools since the last session.

   ❏ Reviewed and added new anger triggers and settings to the poster.

2. Anger log

   ❏ Completed the anger log with the addition of an overall rating of anger management success.

   ❏ Encouraged students to continue using their anger logs.

3. Role-play

   ❏ Helped students role-play a difficult situation, using an example from the session.

   ❏ Distributed the Ten Role-Play Questions handout and asked students to refer to it during discussion after the role-play.

4. Individual anger management plans

   ❏ Assisted the class as a whole in coming up with and illustrating a sample individual anger management plan.

   ❏ Encouraged students to develop and illustrate their own individual anger management plans.

   ❏ Helped students share and discuss their plans, stressing the individual differences among them.

5. I also covered the following area(s).

   _____

   _____

   _____

"In Control" Studios

Goals

▷ To encourage students to develop role-plays that illustrate a broad range of anger management techniques

▷ To strengthen students' understanding that anger management plans can and do apply to real-world settings

Objectives

▷ Practicing the full repertoire of anger management skills

▷ Understanding more fully the need to continue developing and using individualized anger management plans

▷ In a small-group format, creating a role-play for videotaping or audiotaping

Materials

▷ Easel pad (or another whole-class format)

▷ Student anger management folders

▷ Anger triggers and settings poster (from the previous session)

▷ Session 7 review sheet (one per student)

▷ Video camera or audiotape recorder

▷ Blank videotape or audiotape

▷ *In Control* Studios Role-Play Instructions (one for each small group)

▷ Final Anger Logs

▷ Connecting activity

    Handout (one for each small group)

    Paper and pencils

    Audiotape recorder/player (optional)

Overview

By this session, many students are able to integrate the previous lessons and manage their anger more responsibly than before the program. There are often lively discussions during the role-plays because, as more students report on more actual situations, the difficulties in managing these situations emerge more clearly and realistically. Despite growing understanding, competence, and participation, you may still have students who believe that fighting is the only alternative or that it is impossible ever to control one's anger arousal. Always respectfully challenge these points of view.

In this session, students will get the chance to work together in small groups to videotape or audiotape one or more role-plays. Students are generally enthusiastic about doing either. If you do not have access to audiotape or videotape equipment, you can still conduct the "studios" by having the groups perform their role-plays before the entire class.

This session is devoted to creating and taping the role-plays; students will have an opportunity to view and analyze the scenes in Session 9. If not all the groups have a chance to be taped in this session, you might use the first part of Session 9 to finish up. It is important to leave time to analyze the role-plays, however, and it may be best to take two meetings to complete the taping.

Leader Script

Review

Greet the students warmly. Distribute the Session 7 review sheet, prepared in advance, and discuss briefly.

Did using the anger log from our last session, the complete anger log, help you remember to choose from among all the anger management tools?

Pause for responses or a show of hands.

How many of you used an anger management tool when you were angry? Which ones were most useful? Raise your hand if you agree that a certain tool someone mentions is also very helpful to you.

Pause for responses, recording them under the following separate categories: "Physiological," "Thinking," and "Behavioral." Tally students' use of each type. If any new anger triggers or settings emerge, add them to the poster.

Session Content

Today, you are working for "In Control" Studios. I'll be asking you to get into small groups and create a scene about a situation someone in your group has faced. We'll then tape as many situations as we can. But first, let's role-play and tape an anger management situation together. Does anyone have a situation we could use?

ROLE-PLAY

Listen to a few volunteers' situations and choose one that will be likely to illustrate a range of anger management tools. By now, students will probably be giving ideas enthusiastically, but in the event they are not, you can use the following scenario.

Some students had difficulty at a party on the last day of school before summer vacation. The trouble started when Kim flirted with Henri's girlfriend, Lynnette. Henri thought this was deliberate and disrespectful behavior on Kim's part. He felt burning mad. He felt the anger in his head and in his arms. He kept thinking that Kim had "some nerve" to embarrass him like this in front of everyone. He also thought he was going to beat Kim up and show him who was the bigger man. Then he remembered that his parents were proud of him because he had not been in any trouble this whole semester: Why ruin his record because of Kim? Besides, he knew Lynette didn't even like Kim. His plan was to talk calmly to Lynette and to ignore Kim's flirtatious behavior. He kept telling himself, "Stay calm!" Lynette was glad to talk to him and be rescued from Kim! His tools worked. He thought he handled himself "Great!"

Divide the class into small groups (no more than four or five per group), and give each group a copy of the In Control *Studios Role-Play Instructions. Assign numbers to the groups (or have groups choose a name for themselves).*

Now I'd like the groups to create their own scenes, and we'll tape as many as we can. While you are developing your scene, be sure to ask yourselves the questions on the instruction sheet. Assign a director and cast your main actor and coactor(s).

The creator is the person whose situation is chosen (often, this person adapts easily to the director role). Assist the groups in choosing a director and actors, if necessary, and work to help them answer each question on the instruction sheet as it applies to their role-play. When a group appears to be ready, let group members rehearse once, then tape their scene. Tape as many scenes as you can.

Closing

In this session, you all did a great job coming up with anger management scenes. While we were taping, I noticed that the situations and the anger management tools you chose to use were very different. In the next session, we'll have a chance to play back these tapes and talk more about these differences.

Collect students' filled-out anger logs, or have students save them along with the review sheet for Session 7. Encourage them to keep using their Final Anger Logs as they experience anger-provoking situations.

Connecting Activity

Music/Language Arts

Give each of the small groups a copy of the connecting activity handout, and encourage them to follow the instructions. Before showing each videotape in Session 9, let one student from the group who created it share the title the group selected, as well as the musical sound track or thematic introduction in poetry or rap.

"IN CONTROL" STUDIOS

Role-Play Instructions

Group number/name _____ Date _____

You are working for *In Control* Studios. You have just landed a high-paying contract to produce a scene to help students learn anger management skills. With your group, write the scene, telling what happens and what your characters say. You may draw your scene as a comic strip if you wish, but if you do you'll need to show what each character says and thinks. *Hint*: In comic strips, artists use small bubbles rising from the character to a larger "speech bubble" when a character is not saying anything aloud.

Discuss and write down the answers to the following questions as you create your scene:

1. How many characters will be involved? Who are they?

2. What is the setting?

3. What anger trigger starts the action?

4. Does your character think the trigger is accidental or deliberate?

5. Where does the main character feel anger in his or her body?

6. How angry is your character (on a scale of 1 to 5, with 5 being the most angry)?

7. What anger management tool or tools will your character use in the scene?

8. What kind of self-talk/self-statement will your main character use as he or she calms down and chooses to use anger management tools?

9. Will your main character meet the criteria for good anger management (stay in control, respect people and property, get positive results)?

10. How well will your character handle the situation (on a scale of 1 to 5, with 5 being the best)?

Note: If your main character does not meet the criteria for good anger management and gets a low overall rating, replay the scene to show better use of the anger management tools.

Connecting Activity

Group number/name _____ Date _____

Your tape for "In Control" Studios has been accepted for viewing at the Academy of Anger Management in Hollywood. However, you just found out they will only showcase your work if it has a musical sound track or poetic introduction. Please select 5 minutes of appropriate music to play in the background to enhance the mood and emotions of the drama of your role-play. If you can, bring in a recording of your selection. If you wish to compose this music, please do so. Record your composition, or be prepared to play it live in class. If you would rather write a rap or poem to introduce the role-play, that would be fine. Be sure to give your work (musical selection, original composition, poem or rap) a title that could also be used as a title for the role-play.

Review

Name _____ Date _____

1. **Anger management tools.** We tallied the number of students who feel a certain type of anger management tool is personally helpful.

   _____ Physiological   _____ Thinking   _____ Behavioral

2. **Anger triggers and settings.** Our class added the following triggers and settings to the poster.

   Triggers

   _____

   _____

   Settings

   _____

   _____

3. **Role-play.** Our class role-played and taped a situation that showed the use of a range of anger management tools.

   Created/directed by _____

   Acted by _____

   Situation

   _____

   _____

   _____

   _____

   _____

   _____

   _____

   _____

   _____

   _____

4. **Anger management plans.** We divided into small groups and used the *In Control* Studios Role-Play Instructions to guide us in developing a number of anger management situations and plans. We taped these and observed some of the differences among them.

5. **Other comments**

   _____

   _____

   _____

Leader Checklist

Leader name _____ Date of session _____

I covered the following topics today *(check all that apply)*.

1. Review

    ❏ Discussed student use of the anger logs since the last session.

    ❏ Tallied students' responses about which types of anger management tools were most helpful.

    ❏ Reviewed and added new anger triggers and settings to the poster.

2. Role-play

    ❏ Role-played and taped a situation that involved the use of a range of anger management tools.

    ❏ Gave each small group a copy of the *In Control* Studios Role-Play Instructions, discussed them, and asked students to refer to them as they developed their role-plays.

    ❏ Taped as many role-plays as time allowed.

3. Anger log

    ❏ Encouraged students to continue using their anger logs.

4. I also covered the following area(s).

    _____

    _____

    _____

Sharpening Anger Management Evaluation

Goals

▷ To further illustrate the range of anger management techniques and anger management plans

▷ To promote critical thinking about and evaluation of responses to anger management situations

Objectives

▷ Sharing and analyzing role-plays that illustrate a broad range of anger management situations and skills

▷ Becoming aware that it is possible to learn from evaluating one's own and others' anger management situations

▷ Consolidating understanding of the need to continue to develop and practice individualized anger management plans

Materials

▷ Easel pad (or another whole-class format)

▷ Student anger management folders

▷ Anger settings and triggers poster (from the previous session)

▷ Session 8 review sheet (one per student)

▷ Video- or audiotape player/recorder

▷ Ten Role-Play Questions (from Session 7, p. 92)

▷ Connecting activity

　Handout (one per student)

　Notebook paper and pencils

Overview

This session is devoted to watching and critiquing the role-plays created by the small groups in Session 8. The groups will enjoy watching one another's performances, whether they are presented in the form of videotapes/audiotapes or performed as live-action scenes. They will all feel like stars!

By this point in the program, most students are very capable of analyzing role-plays, using and identifying all the basic principles of anger management. Even so, continue to list the principles they identify and the positive strategies they see used in the role-plays.

Usually, the discussion of role-plays will be lively: Your main functions will be to keep time and ensure that all of the groups have a chance to share, to keep the discussion focused on the analysis of the role-plays, and to watch for and underscore important points when they arise. Whenever possible, stress the following two ideas: First, that students can learn invaluable lessons from their own and others' experiences in anger management situations and, second, that each situation (and each person's response to it) is unique. Be sure to praise the students lavishly!

Leader Script

Review

Greet the students, and distribute the Session 8 review sheet, prepared in advance. Use the review sheet to briefly discuss the activities during that session. Inquire about students' use of their anger logs, and add any new triggers or settings to the poster.

Session Content

Today we'll have a chance to share the role-plays the groups created during the last session. Let's play the tapes (or enact the role-plays). After each role-play, I'll be asking you to use the Ten Role-Play Questions handout you received in Session 7 to follow up on the scene.

Have group members locate the Ten Role-Play Questions handout in their anger management folders, then share the role-plays. (If everyone wants to go first, determine the viewing order yourself, draw straws, or use some other equitable way of deciding.) Follow the procedure next described.

1. If you assigned the connecting activity for Session 7, have the group play or perform their music, rap, or poem. Play the tape (or have the first group enact their scene).

2. After the role-play is over, ask (or have volunteers ask) the role-play questions of the students who did not create the scene, and encourage discus-

sion. The group who did create the scene can respond and clarify any incomplete or inaccurate answers.

3. Share the rest of the groups' scenes, following Steps 1 and 2 for each.

Once students have viewed all the scenes, make the following inquiry.

We shared a number of scenes today, and each one was different. In what way did you notice that these scenes were different?

Prompt answers on all aspects of anger management: characters, settings, triggers, tools, intentionality, reactions, outcomes, and so forth.

Closing

You've all worked very hard to come up with these great ideas. Does anyone have any special thoughts about the scenes that he or she would like to share with the class? Any thoughts about how a certain scene might have affected you personally?

Sample answers: "It gave me a better idea of how to use my self-statement at home," "I saw how walking away could really help when someone is teasing you," "I liked how the student talked it over with the counselor."

The next session will be our last in the anger management program. We'll take a look at everything we've learned so far and celebrate all our efforts and successes. I look forward to seeing you then!

Collect students' filled-out anger logs, or have students save them along with the review sheet for Session 8. Encourage students to keep using their Final Anger Logs as they experience anger-provoking situations.

Connecting Activity

Language Arts

Give one connecting activity handout, notebook paper, and a pencil to each student. Go over the instructions for the "Things That Bug Me" essay, step by step, allowing students time to jot down their ideas. Help students develop the essay to the best of their ability. Be especially sensitive to those who find writing difficult, whether physically, emotionally, or academically. Consider making dictation a choice.

Connecting Activity

Name _____ Date _____

THINGS THAT BUG ME

Write an essay about the things that make you angry and the way you handle yourself when you are angry. Plan your essay on this sheet. Then write your essay on a sheet of notebook paper. Write one paragraph per section (1, 2, 3).

1. List at least four of your triggers. Include all the things that set you off: the people, the situations, and the things that happen to you. What happened (in one or two sentences)?

   a. _____

   _____

   b. _____

   _____

   c. _____

   _____

   d. _____

   _____

2. Answer these questions about the way you handle yourself when you are angry.

   a. How do you behave when faced with the triggers you have identified?

   _____

   _____

   _____

   b. What anger management tools work best for you?

   _____

   _____

   _____

   c. Have you found a way to change a tool to make it work better for you? If so, please explain.

   _____

   _____

   _____

3. Write what you are proud of doing when you are angry and what you hope to be able to handle even better in the future.

   a. What are you proud of doing when angry?

   _____

   _____

   b. What could you do better? (Everyone can do at least a *little* better!)

   _____

   _____

SHARPENING ANGER MANAGEMENT EVALUATION

Review

Name _____ Date _____

1. **Anger triggers and settings.** Our class talked about use of the anger logs since the last session and added the following triggers and settings to the list.

   Triggers

   _____

   _____

   Settings

   _____

   _____

2. **Role-plays.** We watched the role-play situations the small groups developed last time, using the Ten Role-Play Questions handout from Session 7 to talk about each. We observed the following about the different role-plays:

   _____

   _____

   _____

   _____

   _____

   _____

   _____

3. **Special thoughts.** Members of the class described special thoughts they had about the scenes. Here are some of the things people said:

   _____

   _____

   _____

   _____

   _____

   _____

   _____

   _____

4. **Other comments**

   _____

   _____

   _____

Leader Checklist

Leader name _____ Date of session _____

I covered the following topics today (*check all that apply*).

1. Review

    ❏ Discussed student use of the anger logs since the last session.

    ❏ Added any new triggers or settings to the poster.

2. Role-play analysis and critique

    ❏ Referred each student to the Ten Role-Play Questions handout from Session 7.

    ❏ Played back each small group's tape for the class to watch (or had the groups act out their scenes).

    ❏ Encouraged students to use the handout to help them analyze and critique each scene.

    ❏ Helped students see the variety of anger management tools used and to notice other ways in which the scenes were different.

    ❏ Invited students to comment about ways a particular scene or scenes affected them.

3. Anger log

    ❏ Reminded students to continue using their anger logs.

    ❏ Let students know that the next session will be the last.

4. I also covered the following area(s).

    _____

    _____

    _____

Review and Graduation

Goals

▷ To give students a chance to review the main principles of and provide feedback about the anger management program

▷ To recognize students for their achievements in anger management

▷ To encourage students to continue using the anger management tools they have learned

Objectives

▷ Experiencing validation for efforts to learn and use anger management skills

▷ Recognizing/remembering that successful anger management depends on the ongoing practice of anger management skills

Materials

▷ Easel pad (or another whole-class format)

▷ Student anger management folders

▷ Anger triggers and settings poster (from the previous session)

▷ Session 9 review sheet (one per student)

▷ Certificates of achievement (one per student)

▷ Another small anger management–related token (one per student; optional)

▷ Refreshments (optional)

▷ Final Anger Logs

▷ Connecting activity: Handout (one per student)

Overview

This last session is devoted to general review and recognition, and validation of students' efforts during the previous sessions to learn ways to keep calm and stay in control. The session is also a chance for students to give you their feedback: If there are things that students particularly enjoyed or that could have been done differently, this is a good time to find out about them. The more you learn now, the better able you will be to develop booster sessions and to serve future groups. In addition, because the questions you ask to elicit students' feedback relate to the session content, the answers and discussion help students in their review of the program.

After students have had a chance to express themselves, the anger management graduation ceremony is held. In this ceremony, each student receives a certificate of achievement. We also encourage you to give each student another small token with which to remember the sessions. This might be a pencil engraved with a student's self-statement, a small trophy for anger management achievement with the student's name, or the like. Be creative—the more personalized the token, the more the student will value it.

This special ceremony not only emphasizes the importance of learning to use anger management skills but is also a chance to single out each student in a positive way, as well as to reinforce a sense of accomplishment in all the students. During the ceremony, celebrate with refreshments, if desired. If you wish, invite the school principal or another staff member in a leadership role to present the certificates.

Leader Script

Review

Greet the students, and distribute the Session 9 review sheet, already prepared. Use the review sheet to discuss that session, then invite students to report on their use of their anger logs. Add any additional triggers or settings to the poster.

As you learned by watching the various role-plays the groups came up with, anger management situations and plans come in many, many forms. Most of you have continued to refine, or improve, your anger management plans. Some of you have even made separate plans for especially difficult situations. You are discovering what works for you!

Session Content

Today is our last meeting, and I am very proud of all of you for learning about anger management. To help me get ideas for future sessions and future groups, I'd like to find out from you how this program has helped and how I might make it better.

Ask the following questions, pausing after each question for a show of hands and/or discussion. Record responses as appropriate.

1. How many of you are continuing to use the anger log?

2. How many of you know when you are angry?

3. Who will volunteer to tell me how they know when they are angry?

4. How many of you know your anger triggers?

5. How many students are using anger management tools?

6. What anger management techniques have worked best for the students in this class (physiological tools, thinking tools, behavioral tools)?

7. What did you like best about the sessions? Least?

8. What aspect of anger management would you have liked us to spend more time on?

9. What else might we have done differently?

Answers to this last question will help you plan booster sessions for the future. If time permits, share one or two "Things That Bug Me" essays, written as the connecting activity for Session 9. You may also collect and post the essays in the classroom.

Celebrate!

Now it's time to celebrate! Because everyone has worked so hard, we are going to have a special ceremony to acknowledge all your accomplishments.

Give, or have the principal or other staff leader give, a copy of the Certificate of Anger Management Achievement to each student. If you wish, you may speak with each student individually and give the student another small, personalized token. Serve the refreshments (optional).

Closing

It's important to keep using your anger management skills so you will remember them and improve your ability to manage your anger. Be sure to refer to your student anger management folders on an ongoing basis to help you review and practice the skills you have learned.

Next time we meet together as a group, it will be for a "booster session." In this session, you'll have a chance to find out how everyone has been doing and to polish up your anger management skills. You have accomplished so much! We don't want you to lose your gains.

When we meet for the booster session, I'll give each one of you a review sheet for this session, and then you'll have a complete overview of everything our class has learned in the program. In the meantime, I will keep providing you with blank anger logs. Continue to use them when you find yourself in anger-provoking situations.

Let students know the date and time of the first booster session and where they may pick up more copies of the Final Anger Log. Also inform students about any plans you have for administering the posttest or conducting any other type of evaluation (see Appendix C). Be sure to complete the review sheet shortly after the session; you will need it to introduce the first booster session.

Connecting Activity

Music and/or Physical Activity

Give each student a connecting activity handout. Briefly review the instructions. Check on student progress in this activity at the beginning of the first booster session.

Connecting Activity

Name _____ Date _____

Don't let your anger build up day to day. Find the type of music or exercise that soothes you after you have had a hard day. Be adventurous! Explore the following (and your own) ideas.

Music

Listen to music you have never paid attention to before. Remember, you can also practice the muscle relaxation exercises while you listen.

Do you like pop music to help you wake up in the morning and classical to relax before going to sleep at night?

Does singing help you relax?

Does playing an instrument soothe you?

What else can you think of?

Physical activity

Do something physical to help you relieve stress.

Does dancing to your favorite music calm you down?

If you have always played basketball for fun, does it help to play it to release anger in a safe way (no flagrant fouls, now!)?

If you have always played soccer to burn off anger, would long-distance running be a good alternative when there is no one to play soccer with?

Does swimming soothe you? Would a shower work almost as well—at least until you can get to a pool?

What else can you think of?

Try three different styles of music and/or ways of being physically active over the next month. On a sheet of notebook paper, write down what you liked and did not like. Place these comments in your anger management folder. Plan to report on your discoveries at the first booster session.

Certificate of
Anger Management Achievement

~

Awarded to _____

on this day _____

_____
Signature

REVIEW AND GRADUATION

Review

Name _____ Date _____

1. **Anger triggers and settings.** Our class talked about use of the anger logs since the last session and added the following triggers and settings to the list.

   Triggers

   _____

   _____

   Settings

   _____

   _____

2. **Review and feedback.** We discussed a number of questions to give us the opportunity to review and give feedback about the program. Here are some of the things we said:

   _____

   _____

   _____

   _____

   _____

   _____

   _____

3. **Celebration and recognition.** Each member of the class received a certificate of achievement. In addition:

   _____

   _____

4. **Anger logs.** We talked about where the anger logs would be and said once again that it is important to continue using them. We also discussed plans for the first booster session and any evaluation.

5. **Other comments**

   _____

   _____

   _____

Leader Checklist

Leader name _____ Date of session _____

I covered the following topics today *(check all that apply)*.

1. Review

   ❏ Discussed student use of the anger logs since the last session.

   ❏ Added any new triggers or settings to the poster.

2. Student feedback

   ❏ Asked questions to solicit student feedback and provide a general overview of program content.

3. Celebration and recognition

   ❏ Distributed (or had the school principal distribute) certificates of achievement.

   ❏ Spoke individually with each student and/or gave the student another small, personalized token (optional).

   ❏ Provided refreshments (optional).

4. Closing

   ❏ Reminded the class that this is the last session; let students know any plans for evaluation and future meetings.

   ❏ Informed students that anger logs will still be available, and encouraged them to keep using their anger management skills.

   ❏ Invited students to experiment with the connecting activity for this session.

5. I also covered the following area(s).

   _____

   _____

   _____

Appendix A

"In Control"
Ten Points in Anger Management

1. Anger is a normal and natural human feeling.

2. An anger *trigger* is a situation or event that sets us off.

3. An anger *setting* is a place where we tend to get angry.

4. An *anger log* helps us reflect on how we handled our anger this time and decide how we might handle it better next time.

5. Anger management helps us *recognize* our anger, *interrupt* ourselves before we behave inappropriately, and then *substitute* an anger management tool.

6. Anger shows itself in our physiology (our bodies). Deep breathing, counting, and muscle relaxation are examples of *physiological tools* for anger management.

7. What we think to ourselves has an effect on how angry we get. Self-talk and self-statements are *thinking tools* for anger management.

8. What we choose to do can help us stay calm and in control. Walking away or talking things out with a friend are examples of *behavioral tools* for anger management.

9. When we manage anger well, we stay in control, respect people and property, and get positive results.

10. Anger management helps us make our anger work for us: We think ahead and make plans to stay calm and in control.

Anger Triggers and Settings

Triggers

Someone hits or kicks me.

Someone makes fun of me (height, weight, family, speech, other).

Someone talks about me behind my back.

Teacher gives me too much homework.

Someone curses at me.

Someone tries to steal my boyfriend/girl-friend.

Someone tells my secrets.

Someone steals from me.

Someone brags too much.

Someone manipulates me.

Someone tells lies/rumors *about* me.

Someone tells lies/rumors *to* me.

Someone blames something on me.

I have to go to classes I don't like.

Someone criticizes me or my work.

I feel cheated.

Someone takes the fun out of things.

Someone embarrasses me.

Someone repeats what I say/mimics me.

Someone ignores me.

I don't get something I need.

Someone does not listen to me.

Someone does not trust me.

Someone goes behind my back.

Someone plays with other people's heads.

Someone can't see his or her own faults.

Someone can't tell my feelings are hurt.

Someone threatens me.

Someone talks about my family.

Someone puts me in the middle.

Someone breaks my things.

Someone copies off my test.

Settings

Gym class

Cafeteria

Hallway

Lunch room

School bus

Dinner table

Bowling alley

Math class

Soccer field

Convenience store

Scout meeting

Relative's house

Choir

Recreation center

Playground

Locker room

On my block

Mall

Bus stop

Procedures for Role-Playing

The following information and instructions apply to all role-plays, beginning with Session 3.

Role-players

Creator/director: The student who volunteers to describe the situation is the creator. His or her job is to choose a main actor and coactor(s), and to give enough detail about the situation so these actors can perform the role-play. Most commonly, the creator also serves as director. To start and stop action during the role-play, the creator/director says, "action" and "cut," accompanied by a handclap or the use of a real director's clapboard. (The clapboard adds realism and gives the job more importance.)

Actor(s): The creator/director chooses a main actor and as many coactors as are needed to role-play the situation.

Observers: The other class members are observers. Their job is to watch during the role-play and be prepared to give constructive feedback afterward.

Setting up the role-play

1. Ask for a volunteer (the creator/director) to describe a situation to role-play. The situation may illustrate good anger management or anger mismanagement.

2. Encourage the creator/director to choose a main actor and coactor(s) for the scenario. Ask the following questions to help the creator/director describe the situation.

   ▷ What was your anger trigger?

   ▷ Was the event that set you off accidental or deliberate?

   ▷ What was the setting?

3. Ask the main actor and coactor(s): "Do you think you have enough information to act out this situation?" If yes, proceed. If no, continue to inquire until the situation is clear.

4. Instruct the other class members (the observers) to watch carefully and be prepared to give their feedback.

Conducting the role-play

5. Cue the creator/director to begin the scene by using the clapboard and calling "action."

6. Have the main actor and coactor(s) enact the role-play. Redirect the actors if you feel the role-play is getting off track. If the creator/director has chosen a situation in which he or she has mismanaged anger:

   ▷ Prompt the creator/director to call "cut" at a point of heightened arousal but before the situation becomes out of control.

   ▷ Have the role-players reenact the situation from the beginning, this time using good anger management, especially the anger management tool(s) identified in the session.

7. When the role-play is complete, have the creator/director use the clapboard and call "cut."

Processing the role-play

8. Ask the specific processing questions given in each session.

9. Elicit responses and feedback from everyone in the group, giving your own feedback last.

10. Praise the creator/director, actor(s), and observers for their efforts.

Booster Sessions

Ideally, by this time, you, your students, and other school staff will have been able to integrate the *In Control* program into the larger school culture. Booster sessions allow you to reinforce the basic principles of the program, encourage students to use the anger log, and help them track their growing use of positive coping strategies when angry. In these ways, booster sessions reinforce previous and support further skill development. Optimally, offer booster sessions every other week for the rest of the school year. At a minimum, hold booster sessions once a month.

This appendix includes two sample booster sessions for reviewing and extending the main program. The first session is open-ended, with the focus on review of anger logs and role-playing of current anger management situations in students' lives. You can use this format now—and a year from now. It will always be different and never boring: Students will supply an endless variety of comments for discussion and situations to role-play. (Usually, we find that students continue to enjoy role-playing, a powerful way to rehearse positive anger management skills within an interpersonal context.)

The second session focuses on how alcohol and other drugs negatively affect people's ability to recognize and feel anger, as well as how they limit people's ability to make use of the program's anger management skills and make anger work for them. Not only is this session an important extension of the anger management program, it also makes an excellent addition to drug abuse prevention programs.

We hope these booster sessions serve as models to get you started in creating your own. View them as guides rather than as rigid structures. Respond to your students' current pressing anger management needs. At one time students may need to discuss the use of positive strategies; at another time, they may need more anger management practice through role-playing. Be flexible and vary session content. Flexible sessions are successful sessions!

You will notice that in these sessions no specific reference is made to the anger triggers and settings poster, nor do the sessions include connecting activities. By now, students probably have a fairly comprehensive list of anger triggers and settings. If they come up with more, by all means add them. Now that anger management is more a part of the school culture, if you need ideas for connecting activities you can ask other members of your teaching team, subject specialist teachers, or your curriculum specialist for additional suggestions.

Anger Management Skill Checkup

Goals

▷ To reinforce and provide students with guidance for maintaining and strengthening their anger management skills

▷ To increase the likelihood that students will continue to work to develop their anger management skills

Objectives

▷ Through role-playing, practicing anger management skills in a supportive environment

▷ Strengthening one's resolve to continue to use these techniques in the school, at home, and in the community

Materials

▷ Easel pad (or another whole-class format)

▷ Student anger management folders

▷ Session 10 review sheet (one per student)

▷ Anger triggers and settings poster

▷ Ten Role-Play Questions (from Session 7, p. 92)

▷ Final Anger Log

Overview

This booster session is a generic, "touching base" meeting, involving role-plays that you can easily tailor to your students' current needs and skill levels. Through this session, you can see how well students are keeping up with their anger log use and how they are integrating the anger management techniques into the real world. By this point, students have probably internalized the role-play procedures and follow-up questions. Many classes are now able to conduct the role-plays by themselves with very little help from you.

This session is also an opportunity to discuss with students what aspects of their learning they perceive as valuable in everyday life. Often, you will find that a student still denies the relevance of anger management. Respectfully challenge such a perception—for example, say "Well, Amec, you may say that, but I was very proud of you when you walked away from Thomas when he teased you last week. More important, I hope you were proud of yourself." Remember, reinforcing student self-esteem is extremely important to the continuing success of the program. You may also find that other students will redirect, then praise a negative student for taking a more positive stance. By all means, encourage this!

Leader Script

Review

Welcome students to their first booster session, and tell them how glad you are to focus on anger management again and to have a chance to find out what has been going on with each one of them. Give each student a Session 10 review sheet, then briefly discuss.

Please raise your hand if you have continued to use your anger logs. Does anyone have any new anger triggers or settings to add to the poster?

Pause for a show of hands; record any new triggers or settings.

At this point, what part or parts of the log do you find help you the most? Why?

Record responses and reasons as students generate them. Sample answers: "The part about how well you did so I can work on doing better next time" or "Thinking about what kinds of things set me off." (Sections about anger management criteria and anger triggers, respectively.)

Session Content

From your anger management logs, let's list some examples of positive anger management strategies this class has used since we last met.

Have students describe recent anger management situations and discuss how they used their anger management tools. Record students' responses as they generate them.

Role-play practice solidifies skill learning.

Have students locate the Ten Role-Play Questions handout in their anger management folders.

Now, to get back into the swing of things, let's role-play a situation in which someone used a positive anger management strategy. Practicing your skills through role-playing really helps you remember them and keeps you sharp, just the way practicing your foul shot on a regular basis can make you better at the line or practicing your keyboard can make you better with the band.

Select, or have the class select, a situation to role-play. Have the creator/director assign a main actor and coactors, and instruct the rest of the group to observe carefully. Using the guidelines in Appendix A3, facilitate the role-play process to the extent needed, but allow the class to ask and answer the Ten Role-Play Questions. Comment only if the class misses a truly important point.

After the role-play, praise students for their role-playing and leadership efforts. Be sure to make specific statements, such as "Callie, as creator/director, you did an excellent job of including everyone in creating and running this role-play."

Some anger management issues may need special attention.

What anger-related issues does this class feel need special attention? Let's discuss some of the situations where these issues come up and what plans we might be able to make to deal with them.

Encourage and record student responses. For example:

Juan says that kids on his block continue to call him names, even though he ignores them.

Marita reports that her little sister still takes stuff from her room without asking, even though Marita has talked it out with her.

Boris says he continues to lose his temper during soccer games, even though he's been benched three times and has tried counting to 10.

Between now and our next booster session, I'd like you to be on the lookout for these situations. They could be things that happen to you, or they might be things that happen to someone else in this class, another class, at home, or in the community. Use your anger logs to record the situation and how your plan (or what the other person did) worked out. Be sure to use you anger log to record other anger management situations, too. Always remember that you can use your log to help you control your anger appropriately.

Closing

Class, you did a wonderful job running the role-play and remembered so much about what we have learned throughout the program. I'm really looking forward to our next booster session and to finding out what you observed about the special anger management issues we talked about.

Let students know the date and time of the next booster session and where they may pick up more copies of the Final Anger Log. Remind them to keep all their logs and handouts in their anger management folders.

Review

Name _____ Date _____

1. **Anger log.** Most people in the class are/are not using the anger log *(circle one)*. Our class mentioned these sections of the log as being most helpful.

   Section   *Reason*

   _____

   _____

   _____

   _____

   _____

   _____

2. **Positive anger management.** We talked about positive anger management strategies class members used since the last session.

   Situation   *Strategy/skill(s)*

   _____

   _____

   _____

   _____

   _____

   _____

3. **Role-play**

   Created/directed by _____

   Acted by _____

   Situation

   _____

   _____

   _____

   _____

   _____

   _____

   _____

   _____

   _____

4. **Special issues.** Our class described the following special anger management issues and plans for working on them.

Situation   *Plan*

_____

_____

_____

_____

_____

_____

_____

_____

_____

_____

_____

_____

_____

Leader Checklist

Leader name _____ Date of session _____

I covered the following topics today (check all that apply).

1. Review

   ❏ Checked for continued student use of anger logs.

   ❏ Asked for students' opinions about most useful section(s) of log.

2. Positive anger management use since last session

   ❏ Listed and discussed anger management strategies used recently by students.

3. Role-play

   ❏ Helped students choose a situation to role-play.

   ❏ Encouraged student leadership of the role-playing process.

4. Special anger management issues

   ❏ Discussed pressing anger-related issues for this class.

   ❏ Discussed what plans students might make to work on these.

   ❏ Asked students to use their anger logs to record situations that illustrate these issues.

5. Anger logs

   ❏ Encouraged students to continue using their logs.

6. I also covered the following area(s).

   _____

   _____

   _____

Anger, Alcohol, and Drugs

Goal

▷ To help students learn about the adverse effects that alcohol and other drugs can have on their ability to recognize their anger and manage it appropriately

Objectives

▷ Learning that alcohol and other drugs have a negative effect on one's ability to recognize and control one's thoughts, feelings, and behavior

▷ Understanding that the use of these substances can undermine the success of all anger management plans

Materials

▷ Easel pad (or another whole-class format)

▷ Student anger management folders

▷ Booster Session 1 review sheet (one per student)

▷ Anger triggers and settings poster

▷ Final Anger Log

Overview

Everyone who works with children and youth plays a crucial role in helping them understand the dangers of alcohol and drug involvement. The main objective of this session is to help students understand that, although one of the main goals of the *In Control* program is to get in touch with one's feelings, alcohol and other drugs can do the opposite, resulting in loss of control.

This session only briefly introduces the relationship between good anger management and the use of alcohol and other drugs. Refer any student who wants to learn more about these substances or who may need help with an alcohol or drug problem to the school substance abuse specialist, school counselor, or other appropriate staff for guidance.

Leader Script

Opening

Greet students as they arrive for the session. Give each student a copy of the review sheet for Booster Session 1, then discuss. Add new anger triggers or settings to the poster, if any.

The topic of this session is how alcohol and other drugs affect your ability to use your anger management tools and make your anger work for you. But first let's talk about the anger management issues that we said in our last session needed special attention. Did anyone experience one of the situations? Did anyone observe one? Let's talk about what happened.

Encourage students to describe situations and to discuss how their ideas for dealing with these issues worked out. For example:

Juan reports that he walked up to the kids teasing him and said, "Knock it off. I don't appreciate your calling me names," and they finally stopped.

Marita says that she is still stuck. She is thinking of asking her parents for help but would rather find a way to deal directly with her sister. Any ideas to help her out?

Boris reported that he came up with some effective self-talk and hasn't been benched in a month.

Give lots of praise for continued use of the log!

Session Content

Today we are going to discuss the relationship between anger and the use of alcohol and other drugs. Did you know that alcohol is a drug? *(Students respond.)* It is, just like marijuana, crack cocaine, or heroin. These chemical substances alter the human mind, making it difficult for a person to monitor and control his or her feelings, thinking, and behavior.

Alcohol and other drugs put us out of touch with ourselves.

Alcohol and other drugs change what is happening in the mind. Once they get into your body, your perceptions of what is going on outside you change. Your ability to tell what is going on inside you changes, too. You become out of touch with your feelings. Once you're out of touch, you become unable to work through problems and meet your needs in appropriate ways. Do you think someone who is out of touch can really make a plan to manage anger? Why or why not?

Encourage responses. Stress the idea that alcohol and other drugs put you out of touch, but good anger management puts you more in touch.

When someone takes alcohol or other drugs, it may cause the person to deny, mask, or cover up anger. What would it feel like to cover up anger? What would a person who was covering up or denying anger look like?

> *Pause for and record responses. Sample answers: "Numbed out," "He couldn't remember what happened," "Maybe just sit there and not do anything."*

Different chemical substances have different effects on different people. But some substances are more likely to cause a person to mask or deny anger. Alcohol, heroin, and drugs like benzedrine can cause this type of reaction. Marijuana (especially if used frequently) also tends to make people to feel "zoned" and out of touch.

Other substances tend to have the opposite effect. They may encourage a person to exaggerate or intensify their anger. Cocaine, methamphetamine ("crystal meth"), other stimulants, and sometimes alcohol have this effect. Taking anabolic steroids to get stronger can also make a person very aggressive. What do you think a person who did one of these drugs would feel like? What might the person do?

> *These substances tend to make a person feel very anxious and paranoid. Likely responses would be to lash out at others or destroy property. Sample answers: "She might think everyone is against her," "Blow up in front of everyone and then start crying," "Maybe her heart would be pounding."*

All of these drugs—plus hallucinogens like LSD and designer drugs like "Ecstasy"—can change and distort what the person is really feeling. That can lead to big problems, one of which is anger mismanagement. To repeat, alcohol and other drugs make us lose control—good anger management puts us in control.

These substances negatively affect our bodies, emotions, behavior, and thinking.

Let's think about how these substances may affect you in a broader way. What might the physical effects of these drugs be?

> *Record students' responses. Sample answers: nausea, vomiting, dangerously rapid heartbeat, weight loss (long term), dizziness, headache, extreme fatigue (tiredness), sleeplessness.*

Everyone reacts differently, and there is no way to know how you will react. What changes in emotions and behaviors might you see in a person who uses these drugs?

> *Sample answers: Rage, which might lead to physical and verbal aggression or property destruction. Depression, in which case the person might not be able to do any of the things he or she normally does (go to school, play sports, even get out of bed).*

What thinking problems can these drugs cause?

Sample answers: Bad judgment and bad decisions, being suspicious of others, forgetting things, not concentrating on school work or other life areas.

Finally, what about behavior? Say a person was high in any of the difficult anger-provoking situations you've described throughout our sessions. Do you think that person would be able to use the anger management tools the way you do? What do you think this person might have done instead, and what might have happened next?

Encourage responses and elaborations. Sample answers: "He might have really lost it and then got beat up," "She might have thought something somebody did was on purpose instead of an accident, then got really embarrassed when she sobered up."

Closing

What we found out from our discussion today is that alcohol and other drugs have a negative impact on your ability to stay calm and in control, and to make your anger work for you. If you choose to use these substances, you won't be able to make anger management plans or use your anger management tools to their fullest. The only way to stay in touch with what you feel and think is to keep alcohol and other drugs out of your body. It's a choice.

If you want to learn more about the dangers of alcohol and drugs, or if you think you or someone you know may have a problem with alcohol and drugs, please speak to me.

If you are able, you can talk to students after the session. If you have set times you will be in your classroom, let students know when those are. Provide additional information and, if appropriate, make referrals to the school counselor, substance abuse specialist, or another helping professional.

Let students know the date, time, and topic for the next booster session and remind them where they may pick up more copies of the anger log. Enthusiastically endorse continued use of the log.

Review

Name _____ Date _____

1. **Anger log**

   Our class experienced or observed these situations and reported on how their anger management plans worked out.

   Situation   *Plan outcomes*

   _____

   _____

   _____

   _____

2. **Effects of alcohol/drugs versus good anger management**

Alcohol/drugs	*Anger management*
You get out of touch with your feelings and needs.	You stay in touch with your feelings and needs.
You deny or mask your anger, or you intensify your anger.	You express your anger appropriately.
You lose control.	You stay in control.

3. **Effects on the body, emotions, thinking, and behavior.** Our class named the following effects as being possible in these four areas.

   Body

   _____

   _____

   Emotions

   _____

   _____

   Thinking

   _____

   _____

   Behavior

   _____

   _____

4. **Resources and referrals.** Here are some places we said you can look for more information about or get help for a substance abuse problem.

   _____

   _____

   _____

BOOSTER SESSION 2: ANGER, ALCOHOL, AND DRUGS

Leader Checklist

Leader name _____ Date of session _____

I covered the following topics today *(check all that apply)*.

1. Anger, alcohol, and drugs

   ❏ Explained how alcohol and other drugs can lead us to deny, mask, or otherwise cover up our angry feelings.

   ❏ Discussed how alcohol and other drugs can lead us to exaggerate or intensify our anger.

2. Our feelings and good anger management

   ❏ Explained that alcohol and other drugs put us out of touch with our feelings; anger management puts us in touch.

   ❏ Alcohol and other drugs make us lose control; positive anger management tools put us in control.

3. Effects

   ❏ Reviewed the possible effects of specific substances.

   ❏ Reviewed the effects of alcohol and other drugs on the body, emotions, thinking, and behavior.

4. Substance abuse resources and referrals

   ❏ Let students know how they can get more information about alcohol and other drugs, as well as help for problems with substance abuse.

5. Anger log

   ❏ Encouraged students to continue using their logs.

6. I also covered the following area(s).

   _____

   _____

   _____

Program Evaluation

There are a number of ways to evaluate the effectiveness of the *In Control* program.

Comparing the essays written as connecting activities for Session 9 with those from Session 1 is an effective tool for authentic assessment. If possible, have each student help make this comparison and assessment through short individual conferences.

If portfolio assessment is used at your school, you may wish to add these two written assessments to the student's portfolio, giving future staff members valuable insights into the student's social development. Criteria can also be developed to analyze the student's anger logs as a part of portfolio assessment.

Factor in any feedback students have given you about the program, either given during Session 10 or informally. You might want to hold roundtable discussions of the program after Session 10, in which smaller groups of students can offer specific comments.

As mentioned in the introduction, we recommend that you use the instrument here to administer a pretest and posttest to each student. Pretests should be given a week or so before the program's first session. Posttests should be given after the last session of the core program (Session 10), preferably within 2 weeks. Compare students' scores on these two tests; enter the scores into school records where appropriate.

"IN-CONTROL" ANGER MANAGEMENT PRETEST/POSTTEST

Name _____ Date _____

Answer the following questions the best you can.

1. We call the incidents that spark our anger:

   ❏ a. litmus ❏ d. resolutions

   ❏ b. triggers ❏ e. physiology

   ❏ c. ammunition

2. We say someone is successfully using good anger management skills when they:

   ❏ a. talk things out ❏ d. hit someone

   ❏ b. throw an object ❏ e. threaten someone

   ❏ c. plan to retaliate ("get back at")

3. Anger is a normal human feeling. ❏ true ❏ false

4. Check *two* examples of the physiology of anger.

   ❏ a. sweaty palms ❏ c. tense muscles

   ❏ b. crooked elbow ❏ d. sprained ankle

5. If someone who is angry manages to stay calm, respect people and property, and get positive results, we would say *(circle one)*:

   ❏ a. The person did not handle the situation well.

   ❏ b. The person handled the situation well.

   ❏ c. The person is a wimp.

6. Name *two* things that tend to get you angry.

   a. _____

   b. _____

7. Name *two* positive ways of handling angry feelings.

   a. _____

   b. _____

Decide how well the following three situations were handled: Write a plus sign (+) if you think the situation was handled well. Write a minus sign (-) if you don't think it was handled well.

8. _____ When Sara felt too angry, she asked for permission to leave the classroom for a few minutes.

9. _____ While standing in line at the school cafeteria, Maggie punched Gerald in the back because he called her a name.

10. _____ Sam ignored Rikki's threats and calmly walked away.

Score _____

PRETEST/POSTTEST SCORING KEY

SCORING

▷ Each test question is worth 10 points, for a total of 100.

▷ Questions 1, 2, 3, 5, 8, 9, and 10: For these, there is only one correct answer.

▷ Question 4 is a multiple choice question with two correct responses, worth 5 points each. If an incorrect response is given with a correct response, ignore the incorrect response, but give the student five 5 points credit for the one correct response.

▷ Questions 6 and 7 also have two parts that are worth 5 points each; accept any reasonable answers for these.

ANSWERS

1. b—Triggers

2. a—Talk things out

3. True

4. Sweaty palms; tense muscles

5. b—The person handled the situation well.

6. Answers will vary. Any examples of behaviors that could provoke a person's anger are acceptable.

7. Answers will vary. Any examples of nonviolent, prosocial behaviors that avoid negative outcomes are acceptable.

8. Sara (+)

9. Maggie (-)

10. Sam (+)

Organizing a Schoolwide Nonviolence Week

Teaching a class or two of students to manage their anger better is a good start, but it is even more important to encourage the development and use of good anger management skills throughout the entire school. Toward this end, and as explained in the book's introduction, it is vital that all school staff learn how to encourage effective anger management and that all students be exposed to the basic anger management program.

This appendix offers suggestions for promoting successful anger management through an intense week of schoolwide attention to this essential life skill. Specific goals for this school nonviolence week are as follows:

> ▷ To promote awareness of and interest in successful anger management

> ▷ To reinforce anger management skills in individual students

> ▷ To establish and/or strengthen a school culture of nonviolence

Organizing the Week

Form a committee, representing students, staff, parents, and administration. Ask for volunteers through school newsletters and by posting notices. Direct the committee to do as follows:

> ▷ Select a date for a schoolwide nonviolence week. This special week should take place after students have completed the core sessions of the *In Control* program (Sessions 1 through 10).

> ▷ Plan the specifics of the nonviolence week while the core program is running.

> ▷ Publicize the upcoming week by circulating flyers, making announcements, and posting information on school bulletin boards.

> ▷ Encourage all school staff and students to be creatively involved.

Specific Suggestions

For the Classroom

Invite classroom teachers to plan the way in which they will participate. Encourage every teacher to teach at least one special lesson during this week on nonviolence. Here are some ideas:

1. Use the Internet to begin sharing your class activities in anger management with other schools and learning about similar activities in other schools.

2. Read a special play or story that demonstrates the link between appropriate anger management and nonviolence.

3. Encourage students to write a story with the theme of nonviolence.

4. Take another look at either a historical or current event that focuses on the connection between positive anger management skills and nonviolence.

5. Decorate the class bulletin board (or a central school mural) according to the theme of nonviolence. Here are some examples of items you could post, but feel free to come up with your own ideas:

   The "Things That Bug Me" essays (see Session 9)

   Student posters, poetry, essays, and artwork illustrating the importance of tolerating others' differences

   Students' personal self-statements

For the Whole School

Beyond the classroom, try using some of these ideas:

1. Run a schoolwide art contest for drawings that emphasize an anger management or nonviolence theme. Give awards to the winners—for example, a gift certificate to a favorite fast-food restaurant.

2. Consider holding a schoolwide assembly with an appropriate outside speaker to discuss nonviolence.

3. If your school has a lunchroom, consider changing the names of food items on your menu to ones with a message of nonviolence: Peaceful Pizza, Keep it Cool Quiche, Talk It Out Tuna Casserole. Ask your students to help come up with the names.

4. During a school assembly, show several of the videos that students have made (see Sessions 8 and 9). Play the sound tracks—perform poems or raps.

5. Let the students design and paint T-shirts or sweatshirts with their favorite self-statements (staff, too!). Choose a special day during the nonviolence week when everyone wears one of the shirts. Give everyone who does wear a shirt free dessert that day at the cafeteria.

6. Put out a special issue of the school newspaper with a focus on all the nonviolence activities: Print poems, raps, the "Things That Bug Me" essays (see Session 9), and interviews with students about what nonviolence means to them.

7. Include a page on the nonviolence week in your school's yearbook.

8. In gym classes, tie the concepts of anger management and nonviolence to the idea of being a good sport.

References
and Selected Bibliography

Beck, R., & Fernandez, E. (1998). Cognitive-behavioral therapy in the treatment of anger: A meta-analysis. *Cognitive Therapy and Research, 22,* 63–74.

Conners, C. K. (1989). *Manual for Conners' Rating Scales: Conners' Teacher Rating Scales, Conners' Parent Rating Scales.* North Tonawanda, NY: Multi-Health Systems.

Deffenbacher, J. L., Lynch, R. S., Oetting, E. R., & Kemper, C. C. (1996). Anger reduction in early adolescents. *Journal of Counseling Psychology, 43,* 149–157.

Dubow, E. F., Huesman, L. R., & Eron, L. (1987). Mitigating aggression and promoting prosocial behavior in aggressive elementary schoolboys. *Behaviour Research and Therapy, 25,* 527–531.

Etscheidt, S. (1991). Reducing aggressive behavior and improving self-control: A cognitive-behavioral training program for behaviorally disordered adolescents. *Behavior Disorders, 16,* 107–115.

Feindler, E. L. (1991). Cognitive strategies in anger-control interventions for children and adolescents. In *Child and adolescent therapy: Cognitive-behavioral procedures,* P. C. Kendall (Ed.). New York: Guilford.

Feindler, E. L. (1995). Ideal treatment package for children and adolescents with anger disorders. In *Anger disorders: Definition, diagnosis and treatment,* H. Kassinove (Ed.). Washington, DC: Taylor and Francis.

Feindler, E. L., & Ecton, R. B. (1986). *Adolescent anger control: Cognitive-behavioral techniques.* New York: Pergamon.

Feindler, E. L., Ecton, R. B., Kingsley, D., & Dubey, D. R. (1986). Group anger control training for institutionalized psychiatric male adolescents. *Behavior Therapy, 17,* 109–123.

Feindler, E. L., Marriott, S. A., & Iwata, M. (1984). Group anger-control training for junior high school delinquents. *Cognitive Therapy and Research, 8,* 299–311.

Goldstein, A. P. (1999). *The Prepare Curriculum: Teaching prosocial competencies* (rev. ed.). Champaign, IL: Research Press.

Goldstein, A. P., Glick, B., & Gibbs, J. C. (1998). *Aggression replacement training: A comprehensive intervention for aggressive youth* (rev. ed.). Champaign, IL: Research Press.

Hinshaw, S. P., Henker, B., & Whalen, C. K. (1984). Self-control in hyperactive boys in anger-inducing situations: Effects of cognitive-behavioral training and methylphenidate. *Journal of Abnormal Child Psychology, 12,* 55–77.

Kellner, M. H. (1997). Weaving anger management into the classroom culture. *Classroom Leadership, 1,* 4.

Kellner, M. H. (1999, April). Children can learn to manage anger. *Healthlinks Newsletter.* (www.Healthlinks.net)

Kellner, M. H. (2000, February). A teen's "anger plan" pays off. *Healthlinks Newsletter.*
(www.Healthlinks.net)

Kellner, M. H., & Bry, B. H. (1999). The effects of anger management groups in a day school
for emotionally disturbed adolescents. *Adolescence, 34,* 645–652.

Kellner, M. H., Colletti, L., & Bry, B. H. (1999, October). *The effects of a classroom-based anger
management program and booster sessions on early adolescents with emotional/behavioral disorders.* Paper presented at the proceedings of the Children, Culture, and Violence
Conference, Columbia University, New York.

Kellner, M. H., Salvador, D., & Bry, B. H. (2001). *The teaching of anger management and the
development of prosocial behavior.* Unpublished manuscript.

Kellner, M. H., & Tutin, J. (1995). A school-based anger management program for develop-
mentally and emotionally disabled high school students. *Adolescence, 30,* 813–842.

Larson, J. D. (1992). Anger and aggression management techniques through the *Think First*
curriculum. *Journal of Offender Rehabilitation, 18,* 101–117.

Lochman, J. E. (1985). Effects of different treatment lengths in cognitive-behavioral interventions with aggressive boys. *Child Psychiatry and Human Development, 16,* 45–56.

Lochman, J. E., Burch, P. R., Curry, J. F., & Lampron, L. P. (1984). Treatment and generaliza-
tion effects of cognitive-behavioral and goal-setting interventions with aggressive boys.
Journal of Consulting and Clinical Psychology, 52, 915–916.

Lochman, J. E., & Curry, J. F. (1986). Effects of social problem-solving training and self-
instruction training with aggressive boys. *Journal of Consulting and Clinical Psychology, 15,*
159–164.

Lochman, J. E., Nelson, W. M., & Sims, J. P. (1981). A cognitive-behavioral program for use
with aggressive children. *Journal of Clinical Child Psychology, 10,* 146–148.

Meichenbaum, D. H. (1975). *Stress inoculation training.* New York: Pergamon.

Nugent, W. R., Champlin, D., & Wiinimaki, L. (1997). The effects of anger control training
on adolescent antisocial behavior. *Research on Social Work Practice, 7,* 446–462.

Omizo, M. M., Hershberger, J. M., & Omizo, S. A. (1988). Teaching children to cope with
anger. *Elementary School Guidance and Counseling, 22,* 241–245.

Presley, J. A., & Hughes, C. (2000). Peers versus teachers of anger management to high school
students with behavioral disorders. *Behavioral Disorders, 25,* 114–130.

Schlicter, J., & Horan, J. J. (1981). Effects of stress inoculation on the anger and aggression
management skills of institutionalized juvenile delinquents. *Cognitive Therapy and
Research, 5,* 359–365.

Wilcox, D., & Dowrick, P. W. (1992). Anger management with adolescents. *Residential
Treatment for Children and Youth, 9,* 29–39.

About the Author

Millicent H. Kellner, PhD, MSW, LCSW, is a licensed clinical social worker and certified educational supervisor who has worked with children in the fields of child welfare, mental health, and special education for almost 30 years. Dr. Kellner is presently Project Development Specialist at CPC Behavioral Healthcare's High Point Schools, Morganville, New Jersey. She developed the school's anger management program, the basis for the *In Control* program described in this book. Presently conducting research on the outcome of special education interventions as well as this program, Dr. Kellner has published several articles and made numerous presentations at professional conferences about teaching anger management skills to at-risk youth.